AI FOR MARKETING PLAYBOOK

PROVEN CUTTING-EDGE STRATEGIES TO EASILY AUTOMATE SYSTEMS, OPTIMIZE CAMPAIGNS & SCALE OUTREACH FOR INCREASED PROFITS

BRIAN DUVALL

CONTENTS

WHY I WROTE THIS BOOK

(AND WHY YOU SHOULD CARE)

After four decades in marketing, from marketing Dirtsurfer extreme sports products to helping over 200 entrepreneurs launch their small businesses, I've witnessed every tech evolution our industry has undergone. I've ridden the wave from print ads to digital marketing and watched social media transform from a curiosity into a necessity. Now, I'm witnessing something that makes all those previous shifts look like gentle ripples.

The AI revolution isn't just another tool in our toolkit. It's a complete reimagining of how marketing work gets done.

My son, Scott, was recently promoted to marketing director at a heavy truck dealership serving the Mid-Atlantic region. Sounds great, right? Except his company then acquired another dealer, instantly doubling his workload without adding a single person to his team. Watching him struggle with twice the campaigns, twice the content needs, and the same 24 hours in a day, I realized his situation perfectly captures what's happening across our entire industry.

Here's the truth nobody wants to say out loud: the traditional way of doing marketing, with its endless manual tasks, linear processes, and siloed teams, is broken. It worked fine when we had smaller channel lists and longer campaign cycles. But today? Forget it. The promise of AI is so open-ended that it can be overwhelming. I struggled so much to get my head around the possibilities that I didn't know where to start. This is the book I wish I had when I started out.

INTRODUCTION

THE NEW MARKETING REALITY

Picture this. You're hunched over your laptop at 11 PM, desperately trying to finish a presentation due first thing tomorrow morning. The customer feedback spreadsheet glares at you from one tab, while three half-finished campaign reports mock you from others. Your coffee's gone cold again, and you're wondering if there's a better way to do marketing than this constant scramble.

If this sounds familiar, you're not alone. I've been there, too, more times than I care to admit.

Let me share a quick story. Back when I was Managing Partner at Smart Business Development, we landed a consulting client who specialized in the Optometry industry. He had big ambitions but a small budget. Here's where things went sideways. We scaled back our proven marketing system to fit within his budget. Big mistake. The campaign limped along, delivering mediocre results that left him feeling disappointed. We learned the hard way that cutting corners on strategy is like trying to build a house with half the foundation; it will eventually collapse.

That experience taught me something crucial: the real problem isn't usually the strategy itself. It's our ability to execute it efficiently and effectively with the resources we have.

WHAT MAKES THIS BOOK DIFFERENT

Look, I get it. Another book about AI in marketing? The shelves (virtual and otherwise) are already groaning under the weight of theoretical frameworks and breathless predictions about the robot apocalypse.

This isn't that book.

This is a practical, roll-up-your-sleeves guide based on real implementation, real failures, and real successes. Every strategy I share has been battle-tested, either by me or by the companies I've studied obsessively while earning my Advanced AI Mastery certification.

Here's what you'll actually find inside...

A Campaign-Based Approach: Instead of throwing random AI tips at you, I've organized everything around the natural flow of a marketing campaign. From initial research to post-campaign analysis, you'll see exactly where AI fits into your existing workflow.

Specific Tools, Not Vague Concepts: When I tell you about using AI for customer research, I won't just say, "AI can help with that." I'll show you exactly which tools and prompts you can use to discover where your audience actually hangs out online or how to prompt ChatGPT to generate buyer personas that don't sound like they came from a business school textbook.

Real Stories from the Trenches: When I was CEO of Dirtsurfer USA, we tried to introduce inline boarding to established sports communities and got absolutely roasted in their forums. We thought we knew our audience, young adrenaline junkies aged 12-25. It turned out that demographic was too worried about looking uncool to even try our product. Our real customers? Men over 30 with disposable income who were looking for their next thrill. That's the kind of hard-won insight you'll find throughout these pages.

WHO SHOULD READ THIS BOOK

Let's be honest about who this is for:

Marketing Leaders drowning in expectations: If you're responsible for delivering more results with the same (or fewer) resources, these AI approaches will help you break through traditional scaling limits. I've been there, trying to stretch every dollar and every hour.

Small Business Owners wearing seventeen different hats: When I was helping entrepreneurs launch businesses through micro-enterprise grants, I saw firsthand how overwhelming marketing can be when you're also the CEO, CFO, and chief coffee maker. AI tools can give you access to capabilities that used to require an entire agency.

Marketing Practitioners stuck in the tactical weeds: If you spend more time formatting reports than thinking strategically, this book will show you how to flip that ratio.

Freelancers and Consultants trying to scale without cloning themselves: These tools let you expand your service offerings without working 80-hour weeks.

Notice who's not on this list? People looking for magic bullets or overnight transformations. AI is powerful, but it's not magic. It requires thoughtful implementation and realistic expectations.

HOW TO ACTUALLY USE THIS BOOK

You've got three options here, depending on your situation:

Option 1: The Full Journey - Read cover to cover if you're planning a complete marketing transformation. Each chapter builds upon the previous one, creating a comprehensive roadmap for AI implementation.

Option 2: The Emergency Room - Jump straight to your biggest pain point. Drowning in content creation? Chapter 4. Can't figure out which channels actually work? Chapter 5. Each chapter stands alone with specific solutions.

Option 3: The Reference Manual - Keep this handy for when specific challenges arise. The prompt templates and case studies work as standalone resources you can adapt immediately.

LET'S ADDRESS THE ELEPHANT IN THE ROOM

Every time I talk about AI for marketing, the same concerns come up. Let's tackle them head-on:

"Is AI going to take my job?"

Do you remember when desktop publishing software first became available? Designers panicked, thinking anyone with a computer could now do their job. What actually happened? Good designers became even more valuable because they could produce high-quality work more efficiently. Same story here. AI handles the grunt work so you can focus on strategy and creativity, the stuff that actually advances your career.

"This sounds expensive and complicated."

When I started using AI tools in 2021, I had the same concern. But most of the tools I recommend have free tiers or cost less than your monthly coffee budget. And complicated? If I can figure it out, trust me, so can you. We're talking about tools designed for marketers and small business owners, not engineers.

"How do I know this isn't just hype?"

Fair question. Here's a real example: One of our agency clients, a wedding venue, generated $72,000 in new bookings from a $50 Facebook ad campaign. How? By analyzing successful wedding marketing campaigns and identifying hyper-specific targeting parameters, we would never have thought of ourselves. That's not hype; that's a 1,440x return on ad spend.

A NEW WAY OF THINKING

Here's the mindset shift that took me the longest to grasp: AI isn't about replacing human creativity or judgment. It's about amplifying what you're already good at.

Think of it this way. When I was Director of Public Relations at the Virginia Credit Union League, I developed automated systems that got 95% of our member credit unions to complete a major industry initiative. Did automation replace relationship building? No, it freed me to focus on the high-touch interactions that really mattered while ensuring consistent execution across the board.

The marketers who will thrive aren't those with the biggest budgets or teams. They're the ones who learn to dance with AI, leading when human insight is needed and following when AI can execute better and faster.

WHAT'S REALLY AT STAKE

During my tenure overseeing nearly 100 cold callers at SalesHive, I witnessed firsthand the consequences of teams failing to adapt to evolving technology. The callers who embraced our AI-powered conversation intelligence tools consistently outperformed those who insisted on "the old way." The difference wasn't in skill or experience; it was in adaptability.

The same dynamic is currently playing out across marketing. While some teams still manually copy and paste data between spreadsheets, others are using AI to analyze customer sentiment across thousands of conversations in just minutes. While some writers craft every social post from scratch, others use AI to generate dozens of variations based on proven viral frameworks.

The gap between these two groups is widening every day.

LET'S GET STARTED

Throughout this book, I'll share what I've learned from my own successes and failures, including helping launch over 200 small businesses, earning the Saatchi & Saatchi Mexico commercial spot for Dirtsurfer, and, yes, from the campaigns that completely face-planted.

You'll discover how to use AI to:

- Uncover where your actual customers hang out online (hint: it's probably not where you think)
- Create content that sounds like you, not a robot
- Build email sequences that actually get opened
- Turn marketing data into stories that make sense to your boss
- Scale what's working without hiring an army

But most importantly, you'll learn how to think about AI as a partner, not a threat. Because that's what it really is, the best junior marketing hire you'll ever make, one that never sleeps, never complains, and gets better every single day.

Ready to solve marketing's toughest challenges together? Let's dive in.

But first, let me ask you something: Where are you starting from? Because the path forward looks different depending on whether you're just beginning to explore AI or already neck-deep in implementation. That's why I've included the AI Marketing Maturity Model up next; consider it your GPS for this journey.

AI MARKETING MATURITY MODEL

FINDING YOUR STARTING POINT AND CHARTING YOUR COURSE

Remember when GPS first came out? Half the time, it tried to drive you into a lake, but at least you knew where you were. That's how I felt when I first started implementing AI in marketing; lots of potential wrong turns, but desperately needing to know my current location.

After working with hundreds of businesses through our agency and chamber programs, I've noticed that organizations typically fall into one of five stages when it comes to AI marketing maturity. Knowing which stage you're in helps you focus on the right priorities instead of trying to do everything at once.

Let me walk you through each stage, and I bet you'll recognize yourself in one of them.

Stage 1: The Explorer (Just Getting Started)

This was me in 2023, staring at ChatGPT as if it were some alien technology. If you're here, you're probably:

- Curious about AI but overwhelmed by the options
- Still doing everything manually (and feeling the pain)
- Worried about making expensive mistakes
- Hearing success stories and wondering if they're real

Your next moves:

- Pick ONE repetitive task that annoys you (for me, it was writing meta descriptions)
- Try the free version of ChatGPT or Claude for a week
- Document what works and what doesn't
- Share a win with your team to build momentum

Timeline to next stage: 3-6 months if you stay consistent

Stage 2: The Builder (Creating Your Foundation)

This is where things get interesting. You've had some wins and you're ready to build real systems. At this stage:

- You're using 2-4 AI tools regularly
- Some tasks are becoming automated
- Quality is inconsistent but improving
- Team adoption is uneven

I remember hitting this stage at Saleshive. We were using AI for our knowledge base and script creation, but every piece needed heavy editing because we hadn't developed good prompts yet.

Common frustrations:

- "Why does the AI nail it sometimes and completely miss other times?"
- "How do I get Bob from accounting to stop being afraid of ChatGPT?"
- "Which metrics actually matter?"

Your focus areas:

- Create prompt templates for repetitive tasks
- Set up basic quality checks
- Connect at least two tools (like ChatGPT + your email platform)

- Measure time saved, not just output created

Timeline to next stage: 4-8 months

Stage 3: The Integrator (Making It All Work Together)

This is where the magic happens. Instead of using AI tools in isolation, they start talking to each other. You know you're here when:

- AI touches multiple parts of your marketing workflow
- You have automated sequences running without daily oversight
- Data flows between systems (mostly) smoothly
- Your team asks, "How can AI help with this?" instead of "Do we have to use AI?"

A real example: When AI Actually Reads Your Customers' Minds

Here's a story that perfectly illustrates why the future belongs to companies that let AI handle the heavy lifting. A B2B SaaS company was struggling with the classic sales problem: tons of leads, but terrible conversion rates. Their sales team was drowning in follow-ups, sending generic emails that felt like spam.

Then they did something smart. Instead of hiring more salespeople, they connected their CRM to SuperAGI's AI automation platform and let the machines do what they do best; find patterns and act on them instantly.

Here's what happened:

The AI became their best salesperson: Every time someone downloaded a whitepaper or clicked a link, the AI instantly analyzed their company size, industry, and behavior patterns, then crafted a personalized follow-up sequence that felt genuinely relevant.

No more "spray and pray" emails: Instead of generic blasts, each lead got messaging tailored to their specific needs and interests, automatically, without anyone lifting a finger.

Perfect timing, every time: The system sent follow-ups at exactly the right moments, with exactly the right content, ensuring no lead fell through the cracks.

The results? A 20% jump in conversion rates. But the real win was freeing up their sales team to focus on closing deals instead of writing emails.

The Lesson: Your leads are telling you exactly what they want through their actions. AI can listen, understand, and respond instantly, while your competitors are still crafting their first follow-up email.[1]

Key milestones:

- Integrated workflows across 4+ marketing functions
- 40-60% efficiency improvement (yes, really)
- Custom AI solutions for your specific needs
- Team members solving their own AI challenges

Timeline to next stage: 6-12 months

Stage 4: The Optimizer (Advanced Capabilities)

At this stage, you're not just using AI, you're pushing its boundaries. This includes:

- Predictive analytics driving campaign decisions
- Custom-trained AI models for your brand voice
- Real-time optimization based on AI insights
- Clear competitive advantages from your AI capabilities

For marketers who have reached Stage 4, the results are mind-blowing. AI-driven lead scoring systems can now predict conversion probability with 82% accuracy.

What you're doing differently:

- Building proprietary AI applications
- Creating predictive models for campaign performance
- Using AI insights to spot opportunities competitors miss

- Teaching others in your industry

Timeline to next stage: 12-18 months

Stage 5: The Innovator (AI-First Marketing)

This is the promised land, where AI isn't just a tool but fundamental to how you think about marketing. Organizations here are:

- Industry leaders that others try to copy
- Creating new business models enabled by AI
- Contributing to the advancement of AI marketing practices
- Building sustainable competitive moats

The reality check: Very few organizations are fully at Stage 5 across all marketing functions. But those who are? They're the ones grabbing market share while competitors scramble to catch up.

TAKING YOUR MATURITY ASSESSMENT

Ok, time for some honest self-reflection. Rate yourself 1-5 in each area:

Technology Adoption 1 = No AI tools 3 = Multiple integrated tools 5 = Cutting-edge AI driving innovation

Process Integration

1 = AI for isolated tasks 3 = AI across multiple functions 5 = AI-first process design

Team Capability 1 = Limited knowledge, high resistance 3 = Solid competency across team 5 = Organization-wide AI fluency

Data and Analytics 1 = Basic analytics 3 = Integrated data systems 5 = AI-driven data strategies

Strategic Alignment 1 = Random AI experiments 3 = AI aligned with objectives 5 = AI fundamental to strategy

Innovation Capacity 1 = Following others 3 = Experimenting with new applications 5 = Creating industry-leading innovations

Your total score:

- 6-12: Stage 1 (Explorer)
- 13-18: Stage 2 (Builder)
- 19-24: Stage 3 (Integrator)
- 25-30: Stage 4 (Optimizer)
- 31-36: Stage 5 (Innovator)

COMMON PROGRESSION CHALLENGES (AND HOW TO OVERCOME THEM)

The Uneven Development Trap

This hit us hard at the agency. We were Stage 4 in content creation but still Stage 1 in analytics. The result? Beautiful content with no idea if it was working.

Solution: Focus on your weakest link. It's tempting to focus on areas where you're strong, but balanced development pays off more.

The Integration Plateau

Many organizations get comfortable at Stage 3. The tools work, efficiency is up, so why push further?

Solution: Set specific advancement goals. Challenge your team: "What would need to be true for us to cut campaign development time in half again?" That question unlocks new possibilities.

The Speed Trap

Trying to jump from Stage 1 to Stage 4 is like teaching someone to drive in a Formula 1 race. I've seen it crash and burn too many times.

Solution: Respect the fundamentals. Each stage builds critical capabilities for the next. Skipping stages means shaky foundations.

YOUR 90-DAY QUICK START, BASED ON YOUR STAGE

If you're Stage 1:

- Week 1-2: Daily ChatGPT practice (15 min/day)
- Weeks 3-4: Apply to one marketing task
- Weeks 5-8: Create templates and document wins
- Weeks 9-12: Expand to a second tool, train a colleague

If you're Stage 2:

- Month 1: Audit current tools for integration opportunities
- Month 2: Create a comprehensive prompt library
- Month 3: Implement your first multi-tool workflow

If you're Stage 3+:

- Focus on your biggest gap from the assessment
- Invest in advanced training for your team
- Start building proprietary solutions

THE BOTTOM LINE

Here's what I learned the hard way: Your AI maturity stage isn't a badge of honor or shame, it's just your current GPS coordinates. What matters is movement.

When I started at Stage 1, I felt like everyone else was already at Stage 5. Most were just Stage 2, but with better marketing. Don't let comparison steal your momentum.

Remember, you want to get comfortable with AI tools so that they automate your tedious processes and increase your profits while reducing your workload. Try using AI for member communications, project planning, and social media. That's the real prize, not reaching Stage 5, but finding the sweet spot where AI amplifies your strengths and eliminates your frustrations.

Ready to start implementing? The next chapter will show you exactly how to choose your first AI tools without getting overwhelmed or overspending. Spoiler alert: You probably don't need that $500/month enterprise platform... yet.

GETTING STARTED WITH AI MARKETING TOOLS: YOUR 30-DAY QUICK START GUIDE

The email arrives at 4:47 PM on a Friday (because of course it does). Your biggest client wants a "quick revision" to their entire Q4 marketing strategy by Monday morning. Three months of planning need to be reimagined in a single weekend.

This is your moment of truth with AI tools.

Here's what I wish someone had told me when I was starting out...

THE THREE BARRIERS EVERYONE FACES (YES, EVEN YOU)

Barrier 1: Fear of the Unknown

When I first saw AI-generated content, my gut reaction was, "Well, there goes my career." Sound familiar?

Here's what that fear really is: loss of control. We marketers pride ourselves on creativity and strategic thinking. The idea that a machine could do part of our job feels threatening.

But remember when email marketing platforms first emerged? Marketers worried those new tools would eliminate the need for campaign specialists. Instead, they freed us from mail merges so we could focus on strategy. AI is the same evolution, just on a larger scale.

The mindset shift: Think of AI as the world's most eager intern, brilliant at certain tasks, but needs lots of guidance and never asks for vacation time.

Barrier 2: Analysis Paralysis

My inbox is flooded with "revolutionary AI tools" every day. Jasper, Copy.ai, Writesonic, Rytr, Peppertype, Mindpal, String, Vocable... the list is endless and growing. There are more than 1,000 new AI tools in the Text-to-Image category alone.

When I started researching AI tools I was immediately overwhelmed. I spent three weeks comparing features in spreadsheets. You know what I accomplished in those three weeks? Absolutely nothing. Zero. Nada.

The breakthrough: Stop trying to find the perfect tool. Start with one that solves your biggest headache right now.

Barrier 3: The "It's Complicated" Myth

True story: Phoenix Legal, a mid-sized law firm, insisted AI was "too technical" for their team. These are people who routinely navigate complex legal databases and case management systems.

Two weeks later, their paralegal was using ChatGPT to draft client communications 70% faster. What changed? They started with simple, specific tasks instead of trying to "implement AI" as some abstract concept.

THE REALITY CHECK

The partners at Phoenix Legal had every excuse ready: AI would be disruptive, require advanced technical skills, and confuse their staff. They avoided it altogether.

Then something interesting happened. A new paralegal was drowning in routine client update emails. Same information, slightly different cases, mind-numbing repetition. Sound familiar?

Instead of attempting a firm-wide AI rollout, they tried something radical: The paralegal started using ChatGPT just for drafting these specific emails.

Week 1: The paralegal tentatively tried simple prompts for client update emails. The results weren't perfect, but they were 80% there.

Week 2: With refined prompts and templates, routine client communications that used to take hours now took minutes. Time saved: 70%.

Here's where it gets interesting. Other team members saw their colleague leaving on time while they stayed late. They started asking questions. Soon, the team was experimenting with AI for:

- Summarizing legal documents
- Drafting intake forms
- Creating standard communications

The partners who once believed AI was "too complicated"? They began exploring automated scheduling and enhanced client intake systems.

The reality: If you can write an email, you can use AI marketing tools. Phoenix Legal proved that starting small with one specific problem can transform an entire team's workflow.[2]

YOUR 30-DAY IMPLEMENTATION ROADMAP

Forget everything you've heard about needing months of preparation. Here's exactly how to get started:

WEEK 1: BUILDING YOUR AI MUSCLES

Days 1-3: The Basics

Pick ONE platform. I recommend Perplexity, Claude, or ChatGPT; each has a free tier that is perfectly adequate for learning.

Your Day 1 assignment (yes, there's homework):

1. Write this prompt: "You are a direct response copywriter with the skills and style of [Insert your favorite Copywriter here]. Help me write 5 attention-grabbing email subject lines for [your actual product/service]. Avoid words and phrases that might flag the email as spam."
2. Take the best one and ask: "Make this subject line more compelling."
3. Then try: "Now make it appeal to [your specific audience]"

Notice what happened? You just learned prompt iteration, the foundation of all AI mastery.

Days 4-7: Real-World Application

Stop practicing and start producing. Choose one of these based on your biggest pain point:

- Social media posts for next week
- Email newsletter outline
- Blog post ideas
- Product descriptions
- FAQ responses

Pro tip: Save every prompt that produces good results. I keep mine in a Google sheet called "Prompts That Actually Work," and it saves me hours every week. I also use the Chrome extension AIPRM for ChatGPT prompts.

WEEK 2: SOLVING AN ACTUAL PROBLEM

Days 8-10: Problem Identification

List every marketing task that makes you think, "Ugh, not this again." For me, writing image alt text is necessary for SEO, but it's mind-numbingly boring.

Your problem should be:

- Repetitive (you do it at least weekly)
- Time-consuming (takes 30+ minutes)
- Formulaic (follows a pattern)
- Important (actually impacts results)

Days 11-14: Solution Development

Here's a framework that I find particularly useful:

1. **Document your current process** - What steps do you take?
2. **Create a prompt template** - Turn those steps into AI instructions
3. **Test with real examples** - Use actual work, not hypotheticals

4. **Refine based on results** - AI output is rarely perfect on your first attempt
5. **Build your workflow** - How will this fit into your routine?

Real example: My manufacturing client needed customer testimonial requests. Old way: 45 minutes to write personalized emails. New way: AI generates drafts in 2 minutes based on agricultural type and purchase history. Human review and personalization: 5 minutes. Time saved: 85%.

WEEKS 3-4: INTEGRATION AND EXPANSION

Days 15-21: The Multiplier Effect

Now for the fun part, making tools work together. Start simple:

- **AI + Email**: Use ChatGPT or Claude to write content, then automate sending via your email platform.
- **AI + Social**: Generate post variations, then schedule across platforms. Vocable is great for this.
- **AI + Analytics**: Have AI analyze your performance reports and suggest improvements

One of my favorite methods: Using ChatGPT to analyze customer feedback and then feeding those insights back into content creation. It's like having a focus group running 24/7.

Days 22-30: Scale and Systematize

By now, you should have:

- One AI tool you're comfortable with
- One workflow that saves real time
- Actual results to show your team

Time to expand. But here's where most people mess up: they try to AI-ify everything at once. Don't. Instead, do this:

1. Show one success story to a colleague
2. Help them implement the same solution
3. Document the process together
4. Identify the next problem to solve

THE PRICE OF PROGRESS: UNDERSTANDING AI TOOL COSTS

Let's talk about costs, because nobody else seems to want to give straight answers about pricing.

The Real Cost Breakdown

Subscription Models (Per User)

- ChatGPT Plus: $20/month
- Claude Pro: $20/month
- Jasper: Starts at $49/month
- Copy.ai: Starts at $36/month

My take: Start with free tiers. Only upgrade when you're hitting limits regularly.

Usage-Based Pricing

- OpenAI API: ~$0.01-0.03 per 1,000 tokens
- Make.com/Zapier: Based on "operations" or "tasks"

Translation: 1,000 tokens ≈ 750 words. Many marketing tasks use 2,000-4,000 tokens total.

Hidden Costs Nobody Mentions:

- Learning curve time (budget 2-3 hours/week initially)
- Integration setup (one-time, usually 4-8 hours)
- Quality control processes (ongoing, but decreasing over time)

Try This Starting Stack

Based on helping 200+ small businesses launch:

Months 1-2: Free Tier Explorer

- ChatGPT or Claude (free)
- Airtable (free trial)
- One automation tool free tier (Zapier / Make / String / Mindpal / Bolt / Replit)
- Total cost: $0

Months 3-4: Power User

- One paid AI tool ($20-50 / month)
- Automation tool basic plan ($20-30 / month)
- Total cost: $40-80 / month

Months 5-6: Scale Mode

- 2-3 specialized AI tools
- Advanced automation features
- Total cost: $150-300 / month

That's probably less than what you spend on coffee for the office.

PROMPT ENGINEERING

THE SKILL THAT CHANGES EVERYTHING

Here's what took me months to figure out: Prompt engineering isn't about being clever, it's about being clear.

The Five Approaches That Actually Matter

1. Zero-Shot: Just Ask "Write a blog post about email marketing best practices"

When to use: Never for important work. Always for exploration.

2. One-Shot: Show an Example "Write a blog post about email marketing best practices. Here's a similar post I liked: [example]"

When to use: When you have a good template to follow.

3. Role-Based: Set the Stage "You're an email marketing expert who's helped 100+ companies improve their open rates. Write a blog post sharing your best practices."

When to use: Almost always. This one change improved my outputs 10x.

4. Chain-of-Thought: Show Your Work "Let's create a blog post about email marketing. First, outline the key challenges readers face. Then, provide solutions for each. Ask me questions if you need clarification. Finally, add real-world examples."

When to use: Complex tasks requiring logical flow.

5. Structured Output: Define the Format "Write a blog post with:

- Attention-grabbing headline
- 3 main sections with subheadings
- 2 examples per section
- Bulleted key takeaways
- CTA focused on downloading our guide."

When to use: When you need consistency across multiple pieces of content.

THE PROMPT I USE MOST OFTEN

Ready for one of my most-used marketing prompts? Here's my go-to:

"You are [specific role] helping [target audience] achieve [specific goal].

Context: [relevant background]

Task: [exactly what you need]

Requirements:

- [specific requirement 1]
- [specific requirement 2]
- [specific requirement 3]

Tone: [how it should sound]

Please avoid: [what you don't want]"

This structure has saved me thousands of hours. Feel free to steal it.

YOUR FIRST WEEK ACTION PLAN

Stop reading. Start doing. Here's your homework:

Monday: Sign up for Claude or ChatGPT. Write 5 prompts about your business.

Tuesday: Generate content for one real marketing task you have this week.

Wednesday: Identify your biggest time-waster in marketing.

Thursday: Create a prompt template to solve that problem.

Friday: Test your template with 3 real examples.

Weekend: Explore one automation tool. Try to connect it to your AI tool.

Following Monday: Document what worked and what didn't. Share one win with your team.

THE MISTAKES EVERYONE MAKES (SO YOU DON'T HAVE TO)

Mistake 1: Trying to Hide AI Use

I watched a competitor get roasted online for AI-generated content they tried to pass off as human-written. The giveaway? Phrases like "in the ever-evolving landscape of digital marketing" repeated in every piece.

The fix: Edit the AI output to match your voice. Add personal anecdotes. Ask AI to interview you. Be transparent when appropriate. Yes… I used AI to help me research, write, edit and revise this book.

Mistake 2: One Prompt and Done

Your first AI-generated blog post will likely be garbage. That's ok. So will the second. Your tenth? Follow this playbook and you're likely to get published on a major industry website.

The fix: Iterate. Every good AI output is the result of at least 3-5 prompt refinements.

Mistake 3: Ignoring Context

Generic prompts get generic results. "Write about marketing" vs. "Write about how small law firms can use email marketing to reactivate dormant clients." That's a night and day difference.

The fix: Be ridiculously specific. Include industry, audience, goal, tone, and constraints.

WHAT SUCCESS REALLY LOOKS LIKE

Remember Hollie from the fitness studio? She used to spend Sundays planning content for the week. Now she batch-creates a month of content in two hours on the first Monday. Her engagement is up 40%, and she actually has Sundays off.

That's not about the tools. It's about reclaiming your time for what matters: strategy, relationships, and yes, actually having a life outside of marketing.

The AI didn't replace her creativity; it amplified her strategic thinking

YOUR NEXT STEP

Here's the truth: You're going to feel awkward at first. Your initial AI outputs will sound robotic. Your automations will break. You'll wonder if it's worth it.

It is.

Six months from now, you'll wonder how you ever managed without these tools. It's true, but only if you start today.

So, here's my challenge: Before you read the next chapter, complete Day 1 of the action plan. Write those five prompts. See what happens.

Because the best time to start was six months ago. The second-best time? Right now.

Ready to go deeper? Chapter 1 will show you how to use AI to uncover market insights your competitors are missing. I'll also show you some prompts and tools that could have helped me identify a completely overlooked market segment for Dirtsurfer.

CHAPTER 1
STREAMLINING MARKET RESEARCH WITH AI TOOLS

THE FORUM NOTIFICATION popped up at 2 AM. Someone on a longboarding community had just torn our Dirtsurfer post apart, again. "You don't belong here. You're a wannabe who can't handle a real board," they wrote. Ouch.

Three months into taking over Dirtsurfer in the US, we were struggling to gain market share and were reaching out to the wrong audience. We'd assumed young skaters and snowboarders would love our inline board. Instead, they treated us like we'd insulted their mothers.

That painful experience taught me a crucial lesson: assuming you know your market is the fastest way to burn through your budget. However, here's the thing: back then, proper market research meant hiring expensive consultants or spending weeks conducting surveys that told you what people thought they wanted, rather than what they'd actually buy.

Today? AI has completely flipped the script on market research. What used to take weeks and thousands of dollars can now happen in hours for the cost of a lunch.

THE THREE MARKET RESEARCH MOUNTAINS EVERY BUSINESS MUST CLIMB

After helping launch over 200 small businesses, I've noticed everyone struggles with the same three research challenges. AI is turning these mountains into molehills if you know how to use it.

Mountain 1: Actually Finding Your Real Audience

Remember my Dirtsurfer disaster? We spent months marketing to teenagers and twenty-somethings who wouldn't touch our product with a ten-foot pole. Our actual customers? Men over 30 with disposable income, looking for weekend thrills that wouldn't land them in the emergency room.

How'd we finally figure this out? The hard way, by nearly going bankrupt first.

The Old Way:

- Hire a market research firm ($10,000+)
- Run focus groups ($5,000+ per group)
- Survey potential customers (weeks of work)
- Make educated guesses (mostly wrong)

The AI Way:

A boutique candle maker discovered their actual audience using SparkToro. Twenty minutes of work revealed that their ideal customers weren't "women 25-45 who like home decor" (their initial assumption), but rather "urban professionals who follow specific wellness podcasts and shop at Whole Foods."

Here's exactly how they did it:

1. **Started with their hunch**: "People who buy luxury candles"
2. **Fed it into SparkToro**: The tool analyzed millions of social profiles
3. **Found the gold**: Their audience obsessively follows three specific podcasts

4. **Validated with ChatGPT**: Used competitor data to build detailed personas
5. **Tested with micro-campaigns**: Targeted ads to podcast listeners = 3x conversion rate

The kicker? This entire process took one afternoon and cost $50.[1]

Your Move: Stop guessing. Start with SparkToro's free searches to see what your assumed audience actually reads, watches, and follows online. You might be surprised.

Mountain 2: Understanding What Your Competition Is Really Doing

True confession: I once spent two full weeks manually analyzing competitors for a law firm client. Screenshots of every page, spreadsheets of their service offerings, and pricing pulled from phone calls pretending to be a prospect.

Two. Entire. Weeks.

Today, that same analysis takes me about three hours to complete. And it's more comprehensive.

The Competitive Intelligence Revolution

A dental practice was getting crushed by a competitor that seemed to be everywhere, at the top of Google, booked solid, and charging premium prices.

Instead of the manual slog, they:

1. **Ran their site through AI-powered SEO tools**: Found they were ranking for "emergency dental" terms our client ignored
2. **Analyzed their ad strategy**: Meta Ad Library showed they ran video testimonials exclusively
3. **Decoded their messaging**: ChatGPT analyzed their website copy and identified their unique angle, focusing on dental anxiety, not just services
4. **Found their weakness**: Despite strong marketing, their Google reviews revealed consistent complaints about wait times

Armed with this intelligence, they repositioned themselves as the "no-wait emergency dental practice". They saw a 67% increase in new patient inquiries over six weeks.

The Tools That Changed Everything:

- **Crayon**: Tracks competitor changes automatically
- **Meta Ad Library**: See exactly what ads competitors run
- **ChatGPT with competitive prompts**: Analyzes and synthesizes findings
- **Semrush or Ahrefs**: Reveals their entire SEO strategy

Remember: Your competitors are teaching a masterclass in what works in your market. AI helps you take notes at scale.

Mountain 3: Hearing What Customers Really Think (Not What They Say They Think)

When I was at the Virginia Credit Union League, I learned that what members said in meetings rarely matched their actual behavior. They'd nod politely about our new initiatives, then completely ignore them.

Sound familiar?

The same dynamic plays out in every business. Customers say they want one thing, then buy something completely different. Breaking through this "politeness barrier" used to require expensive research firms and carefully moderated focus groups.

THE AI-POWERED TRUTH DETECTOR

Here's a recent example that still amazes me. A SaaS company had launched a new feature and was drowning in feedback; thousands of open-text survey responses and support tickets were piling up faster than their small team could process. Their traditional satisfaction surveys showed decent ratings, so they figured things were going well.

But when they fed all that unstructured feedback into an AI-powered analysis tool, a different story emerged:

One specific feature was causing massive frustration, mentioned in complaint after complaint. The AI spotted the pattern immediately; something that would have taken weeks of manual review to uncover, if they'd caught it at all.

The real breakthrough came when they:

Stopped relying on averages: High-level satisfaction scores had masked a critical usability issue affecting a significant portion of users

Let AI surface the hidden patterns: The analysis tool identified recurring themes and emotional triggers that traditional surveys missed

Acted on insights quickly: Within days, not weeks, they prioritized and shipped a usability fix

Measured the impact: Customer complaints dropped measurably, and user retention improved

The result? A problem that could have festered for months was identified and resolved in days, all because AI helped them actually hear what their customers were saying.[1]

The Lesson: Your customers are constantly telling you how to improve your business. AI helps you actually hear them.

FROM DATA TO DECISIONS: THE QATALOG TRANSFORMATION

Let me share a story that perfectly captures why AI revolutionizes market research.

A consumer electronics brand (think major player, not startup) had a problem I see everywhere: data paralysis. Their Consumer Insights & Analytics team, four talented analysts, was drowning in information:

- Market share PDFs arriving quarterly
- Customer feedback was scattered across five platforms

- Nielsen data in one format, internal data in another
- Weeks between question and answer

Sound painfully familiar?

By the time insights reached decision-makers, the market had already shifted. It's like driving while looking in the rearview mirror; you'll eventually crash.

Enter Qatalog's AI platform. Instead of replacing the analysts, it became their superpower. The system:

- **Automatically extracted data** from those clunky PDFs
- **Unified everything** into one searchable system
- **Generated insights** in hours, not weeks
- **Scaled across departments** without adding headcount

The results? Analysts stopped being data janitors and started being strategic advisors. Product teams got answers in hours instead of weeks. Market opportunities were spotted while they were still opportunities, not historical footnotes.[2]

LEARNING FROM THE GIANTS (SO YOU DON'T HAVE TO BE ONE)

You might be thinking, "Sure, Brian, but these are huge companies with massive budgets." Fair point. But here's what matters: the same AI capabilities are now available to everyone.

Samsung's Approach: They use AI to analyze customer behavior and optimize everything from store layouts to product recommendations. You can do the same with your website using tools like Hotjar + ChatGPT analysis.

Intel's Method: AI-driven analytics guide their decision-making in real-time. Your version? Connect Google Analytics to Looker Studio and then use ChatGPT to analyze and interpret the trends.

Apple's Strategy: They embed AI throughout their ecosystem for seamless experiences. Your opportunity? Use Make.com, Zapier or AI agents to create your own integrated marketing ecosystem.

The giants are showing us what's possible. AI democratizes these capabilities.

YOUR MARKET RESEARCH ACTION PLAN

Enough theory. Here's your practical roadmap:

Week 1: Audience Reality Check

Monday-Tuesday:

1. List your assumed target audience characteristics
2. Run free SparkToro searches on those assumptions
3. Document the surprises (there will be many)

Wednesday-Thursday:

1. Create ChatGPT personas based on real data
2. Prompt: "Based on people who follow [discovered interests], create a detailed buyer persona including psychographics, daily routines, and purchase triggers."

Friday:

1. Design a micro-campaign targeting your newly discovered audience
2. Budget: $50-$100
3. Measure: Click-through rate vs. your regular campaigns

Week 2: Competitive Intelligence Gathering

Monday:

- Set up Crayon or similar monitoring for the top 3 competitors
- Document their current messaging and positioning

Tuesday-Wednesday:

- Analyze their ads in Meta Ad Library
- Use ChatGPT: "What emotional triggers are these ads targeting?"

Thursday-Friday:

- Mystery shop their sales process
- Feed findings into AI for pattern analysis

Week 3: Customer Truth Mining

Throughout the week:

1. Set up Otter.ai or Hubspot for all customer calls
2. Export all support tickets and reviews
3. Feed batches into Claude or ChatGPT
4. Prompt: "Identify the top 5 frustrations and desires expressed in these conversations."

By week's end:

- You'll have more market insight than most MBAs
- Your assumptions will be validated or shattered
- You'll have clear, data-driven next steps

The Hidden ROI of AI Market Research

Let's talk numbers, because that's what matters to your boss (or your bank account).

Traditional market research for a small business:

- Basic research firm: $15,000-50,000
- Timeline: 6-12 weeks
- Output: One static report

AI-powered research:

- Tools: $100-500/month
- Timeline: 1-2 weeks
- Output: Continuous insights, updated in real-time

But here's the real kicker: the ROI isn't just in cost savings. It's in speed to insight. My wedding venue client discovered that their real customers weren't local brides on limited budgets but recently engaged women from big cities who were looking for the "Old South" fantasy wedding.

One messaging shift. $72,000 in new bookings. From a $50 Facebook ad campaign.

That's the power of knowing your actual market.

Your Biggest Competitor Already Uses AI

Here's an uncomfortable truth: While you're reading this, your competition is probably using AI to understand your shared market better than you do.

The good news? You can catch up in weeks, not years.

The better news? Most of them are using AI badly, generating generic content and calling it "personalization." You're going to use it strategically, starting with actually understanding your market.

COMMON PITFALLS (LEARN FROM MY FAILURES)

Pitfall 1: Trusting AI Blindly

Remember that AI doesn't "think," it predicts the next most likely letter or word in a sequence. This means it will lie or hallucinate. ChatGPT once told me the average small business spends $50,000 annually on marketing. Sounded plausible. It was completely wrong. Always verify claims with actual sources.

Pitfall 2: Analysis Paralysis 2.0

Just because AI can analyze everything doesn't mean you should. I once spent 3 days with a client analyzing every competitor nationwide. That was a big waste of time because 90% of my client's customers came from 5 specific states.

Pitfall 3: Forgetting the Human Element

AI reveals patterns, but humans provide context. When research told us Dirtsurfer customers were "risk-averse thrill-seekers" (seems contradictory, right?), human insight revealed the truth: they wanted the adrenaline experience with lower injury risk than skateboarding.

THE ONE QUESTION THAT CHANGES EVERYTHING

Before you dive into AI-powered market research, ask yourself this:

"What expensive assumption is my marketing based on?"

For Dirtsurfer, it was assuming young people wanted our product. For the wedding venue, it was targeting local brides instead of out-of-towners. For the dental practice, it was competing on price instead of results. What's yours?

Once you identify it, AI can help you test it in days instead of months. And that's when marketing gets exciting, when you stop guessing and start knowing.

Ready to put this into practice? Grab the AI Prompt Cheat Sheet at https://brianduvall.com/ai-marketing-prompts-reference-guide. But first, let me show you how to turn those market insights into positioning that actually converts.

CHAPTER 2
MASTERING BRAND POSITIONING WITH AI TOOLS

"WE NEED to sound more innovative, but also trustworthy. Professional but approachable. Cutting-edge yet established."

The CMO of a tech startup was practically tying himself in knots trying to explain their brand positioning. After 90 minutes of circular conversation, they were no closer to clarity than when they started.

I've sat through hundreds of these positioning sessions. They usually end with watered-down language that sounds like everyone else in the industry. "Leading provider of innovative solutions that deliver exceptional value..."

Kill me now.

But here's what changed my entire approach to brand positioning: AI doesn't carry the emotional baggage we do. It doesn't worry about offending the CEO's ego or protecting sacred cows. Feed it the right inputs, and it'll hand you positioning options that would take a committee six months to maybe, possibly, consider.

WHY MOST BRAND POSITIONING FAILS (AND HOW AI FIXES IT)

Remember when I tried to make Dirtsurfer appeal to everyone who liked board sports? We ended up appealing to no one. Our positioning was essentially "It's like snowboarding, but not! Like skateboarding, but different! Like surfing, but on land!"

The established communities saw right through it. We were trying so hard to fit in that we forgot to stand out.

The Traditional Positioning Nightmare:

- Endless stakeholder meetings where everyone has opinions
- Wordsmithing sessions that drain your will to live
- Generic outcomes that could describe any competitor
- Months of work for messaging nobody remembers

THE AI POSITIONING REVOLUTION

When AI Finally Understood What "Brand Voice" Actually Means

Here's a story that still gives me chills. Brand.ai was watching companies burn through millions of dollars and years of time trying to maintain consistent messaging across thousands of touchpoints. The traditional approach was brutal: hire expensive agencies, create massive brand guidelines, then watch everything fall apart the moment real people tried to implement them.

Then they did something that changed everything. They fed entire brand narratives into Claude and let AI become the ultimate brand guardian.

Here's what happened:

Years of work became instant: What used to take 24 months of agency back-and-forth now happened in days. Claude could process massive brand documents and understand not just the rules, but the soul of a brand.

One copywriter became an army: Instead of hiring entire teams, companies could have a single person manage 600 pieces of content; all perfectly on-brand, all authentically voiced.

The math was staggering: Enterprise clients went from spending $5 million annually on brand compliance to a fraction of that cost.

Agency onboarding went from months to days: New partners could instantly understand and execute brand standards without lengthy training sessions.

But here's the real breakthrough: Claude didn't just follow brand guidelines; it captured the human essence of how brands should sound. As David Corns from Opendoor put it: "With Brand.ai, we can quickly align partners with our brand standards while driving sharper insights, faster briefs, and stronger ideas."

The Lesson: Your brand voice isn't just rules and guidelines; it's the emotional DNA of how you connect with customers. AI can now understand and scale that authenticity in ways humans never could.[1]

Here's how they got there...

THE THREE-PART POSITIONING FRAMEWORK THAT ACTUALLY WORKS

Part 1: Stop Describing, Start Declaring

Most positioning sounds like a product manual. Features, benefits, blah blah blah. Your customers don't care about your "comprehensive suite of integrated solutions."

They care about their problems and their aspirations.

The AI Prompt That Changed Everything:

"You are a brand strategist known for creating memorable, bold positioning statements.

Company: [sustainable fashion brand] Customer problem: Fast fashion guilt but limited budget Our unique angle: Clothes designed to last 10+ years. Competitor positioning: [list their actual taglines]

Create 10 positioning statements that:

- Are 10 words or less
- Make a bold promise or take a stand
- Use concrete language, not corporate speak
- Would make someone stop scrolling

Avoid: clichés, feature lists, trying to appeal to everyone."

Part 2: The Messaging Hierarchy That Scales

Great positioning is just the start. You need messaging that works across every touchpoint without turning into telephone game chaos.

I learned this the hard way at Smart Business Development. Our positioning was solid, but every team member explained what we did differently. Prospects were confused before we even made our pitch.

Building Your Messaging Machine:

Here's the exact process I use now:

1. **Core Position** (the peak): Your 10-word max statement
2. **Three Supporting Pillars**: The reasons to believe
3. **Proof Points**: Specific evidence for each pillar
4. **Channel Variations**: How it adapts by platform

Feed your winning position into this prompt:

"Create a complete messaging hierarchy for [position statement].

Include:

- 3 supporting benefit pillars (one sentence each)
- 2 proof points per pillar
- Variations for:
  - Website headline
  - Email signature
  - Sales conversation opener
  - Social media bio

- Elevator pitch

Keep the core message consistent while adapting tone and length for each channel."

Part 3: Making It Visual (Without a Design Degree)

A positioning statement without a visual identity is like a voice without a face. But most small businesses can't afford custom design work for every positioning iteration.

Enter AI-powered design tools.

The Visual Identity Shortcut:

When a sustainable fashion brand nailed their positioning, they needed visuals fast. Traditional approach? $5,000 and three weeks minimum.

The approach:

1. Fed positioning + target audience into Looka
2. Generated 50+ logo variations in minutes
3. Used Canva's Magic Design with our tagline
4. Created consistent templates in one afternoon

Total cost: $96. Time invested: 4 hours.

Were they as perfect as custom design? No. Were they good enough and immediately usable? Absolutely.

FROM GENERIC TO GENIUS: REAL POSITIONING TRANSFORMATIONS

Let me show you what's possible when you combine clear thinking with AI capabilities:

Case Study 1: Sephora's AI-Driven Beauty Positioning Revolution

Before: Traditional beauty retail model with "common online shopping challenges in the beauty industry" and difficulty differentiating from competitors in an oversaturated cosmetics market.

The Process:

- Partnered with ModiFace and experimented with AR for five years before launching to analyze competitor gaps in virtual try-on technology
- Used AI-powered virtual makeup try-ons to personalize skincare diagnostics and chatbot-driven assistance based on competitive intelligence, showing a lack of personalized digital experiences
- Developed facial recognition technology that detects facial features and applies virtual products in real-time to address competitor weaknesses in product discovery
- Implemented AI-driven recommendation system and sentiment analysis technologies to understand and cater to complex customer preferences

After: "From being just another beauty retailer to a tech-forward, customer-centric beauty destination" with AI-powered personalization as core differentiator.

Results:

- Increased e-commerce net sales from USD 580 million in 2016 to over USD 3 billion in 2022 - representing a 4x increase in online sales over six years
- Customers who used the Virtual Artist tool were 3 times more likely to complete a purchase than those who didn't
- 30% reduction in returns for makeup products and average app session increasing from 3 minutes to 12 minutes
- 25% increase in average order value and 17% rise in repeat customers.[2]

Case Study 2: The B2B Software Breakthrough

Before: "Enterprise-grade solutions for digital transformation" (Corporate lingo bingo, anyone?)

The Discovery: They fed customer testimonials into Claude and found a pattern: clients didn't talk about features. They talked about finally sleeping through the night because the client's software prevented 3 AM crisis calls.

After: "Software that lets IT directors sleep past 3 AM"

Result: Demo requests up 156%. It turns out that specificity sells.

Learning from the Leaders (Without Their Budgets)

The world's top agencies are all-in on AI for positioning. Here's how to steal their strategies:

Pentagram's Approach: They use AI to explore hundreds of creative directions quickly. Your version? Use ChatGPT to generate about 50 positioning angles in minutes, then use human judgment to pick the winners.

Landor's Method: AI analyzes massive amounts of cultural data to spot trends. Your hack? Use Google Trends + ChatGPT to identify emerging language in your industry.

Interbrand's Strategy: They train custom AI on successful brand transformations. Your move? Feed Claude case studies of great positioning and ask it to apply those principles to your brand. The tools cost 1/1000th of agency fees. The results can be just as powerful.

YOUR 5-DAY POSITIONING SPRINT

Monday Morning: The Honest Assessment

1. Write your current positioning (if you can find it)
2. Ask 5 team members to explain what you do
3. Screenshot 5 competitor homepages
4. Note the painful similarities

Monday Afternoon: The AI Deep Dive

Feed this into your favorite AI platform like Grok, Claude, Gemini, or ChatGPT: "You're a brand strategist with deep expertise in competitive messaging. I'm analyzing positioning statements from key competitors in the [industry/category].

Please review the following statements:

[PASTE HERE]

For each, provide:

1. Common clichés or overused phrases (if any)
2. Topics or truths they are collectively avoiding
3. Potential "white space" or opportunity areas not yet claimed

Then synthesize your insights into:

- A summary of messaging trends
- A table of clichés vs. alternatives
- 2–3 suggestions for differentiated positioning angles

Be objective, concise, and actionable. Prioritize clarity over creativity."

Tuesday: The Differentiation Discovery

Interview prompt: "Act as a senior brand strategist experienced in market positioning, customer insight discovery, and narrative differentiation.

I'm going to describe our company, our offer, and what we know about our customers.

Your job is to help uncover a unique positioning angle by asking sharp, probing questions that reveal:

1. What our customers *actually* say or care about vs. what our competitors *assume* they care about
2. The problems we solve that others ignore or underestimate
3. Elements of our approach, story, team, or results that are truly different

Please do the following:

- Ask at least 5 probing questions for each category above
- Identify any missing info you need to help position us effectively
- Then, once I respond, help me explore:
    - Patterns in customer language or sentiment
    - Positioning opportunities (white space) based on what others miss
    - 2–3 rough-draft ideas for unique positioning narratives or taglines

Output your insights in a clear, structured format with tables or bullet points."

Wednesday: Position Generation Day

Use the master prompt from earlier to generate options. But here's the key, generate in waves:

- Wave 1: 20 safe options
- Wave 2: 20 bold options
- Wave 3: 20 weird options

The winner often comes from Wave 3.

Thursday: Message Architecture

Build your complete hierarchy. Test it by explaining your business using only elements from the hierarchy. If you need to add explanations, the messaging isn't clear enough.

Friday: Visual Identity Speed Run

- Morning: Logo explorations with AI tools
- Afternoon: Create 5 templated pieces (email signature, LinkedIn banner, one-pager, slide template, social post)
- End of day: You are well on your way to a complete positioning system

THE POSITIONING PITFALLS THAT AI MAKES WORSE

Pitfall 1: The Thesaurus Trap

AI loves synonyms. Feed it weak positioning and it'll give you back "innovative" becomes "cutting-edge" becomes "pioneering." Still generic, just with fancier words.

Solution: Ban corporate clichés in your prompts. List words to avoid.

Pitfall 2: The Kitchen Sink Syndrome

"We're the innovative, customer-centric, full-service, award-winning, industry-leading..."

AI can combine every input into word salad. More isn't better.

Solution: Force constraints. "Maximum 8 words" or "Must choose ONE primary benefit." Even with these constraints, AI can still gaslight you, so verify the results.

Pitfall 3: The Personality Bypass

AI-generated positioning can sound robotic because, well, it is a robot. Your brand needs human quirks.

Solution: Feed AI your actual customer quotes, team inside jokes, and founder stories. The weird stuff that makes you human.

The Psychology Behind Positioning That Sticks

Here's what most marketers miss: great positioning isn't about being clever. It's about being memorable. And our brains remember:

- **Concrete over abstract**: "Sleep past 3 AM" beats "peace of mind"
- **Unexpected over expected**: "Clothes that outlast trends" surprises
- **Simple over complex**: If it needs explanation, it's not positioning

AI helps by removing our curse of knowledge. We're too close to our businesses to see them clearly. AI has no such baggage.

MAKING THE CASE FOR BOLD POSITIONING

Your CEO, client, or partner will likely push back on bold positioning. They always do. Here's your ammunition:

The Safety Paradox: Playing it safe is the riskiest strategy. When you sound like everyone else, you're competing on price.

The Memory Test: Generic positioning is forgotten in seconds. Bold positioning gets repeated at dinner parties.

The Proof Points: Show them the sustainable fashion brand (300% revenue growth), the dental practice (47% boost), the software company (156% more demos).

Bold positioning isn't risky. Boring positioning is.

Your Positioning Transformation Checklist

Before you move to the next chapter, answer these:

- [ ] Can you explain your positioning in under 10 seconds?
- [ ] Would a customer remember it tomorrow?
- [ ] Does it make competitors nervous?
- [ ] Can every team member say it consistently?
- [ ] Does it guide decisions ("Is this on-brand?")?

If you answered "no" to any of these, you have positioning work to do. The good news? With AI, you can fix it this week, not this quarter.

THE ONE QUESTION THAT MATTERS

Before you prompt AI for positioning help, answer this:

"If we had to bet our entire business on solving one specific problem for one specific group, what would it be?"

Dirtsurfer failed because we tried to be everything to everyone. The sustainable fashion brand succeeded because it chose quality-conscious consumers who hate waste.

Choose your hill. AI will help you plant your flag.

Coming up next: You've got killer positioning, but how do you build a funnel that actually converts? Chapter 3 reveals the AI-powered funnel architecture that turned confused visitors into eager buyers.

CHAPTER 3
OPTIMIZING SALES FUNNELS WITH AI TECHNOLOGY

"OUR FUNNEL IS MORE LIKE A COLANDER."

The SaaS founder's joke hit too close to home. They were looking at their analytics. 10,000 monthly visitors, 500 email signups, 50 trials, 5 customers. A 0.05% visitor-to-customer conversion rate.

I've seen this movie before. Hell, I've lived it. At Smart Business Development, we had a summer camp turned conference center client who built a "sophisticated" funnel with 17 different touchpoints. Know what they achieved? They confused everyone, including themselves.

But here's what nobody tells you about funnels: The problem isn't usually the design. It's that you're guessing about what happens in your prospect's head between "That's interesting" and "Here's my credit card."

AI changes that guessing game into a science.

THE FUNNEL DELUSION WE NEED TO DISCUSS

Traditional funnel thinking goes like this:

1. Awareness → Consideration → Decision
2. Add content at each stage

3. Hope for the best
4. Blame the leads when it doesn't work

I call BS.

Real customer journeys look like a bowl of spaghetti drawn by a caffeinated toddler. They research on their mobile device, abandon the cart on desktop, see a retargeting ad, ask their colleague, forget about you, remember randomly at 2 AM, and then buy on a tablet while watching Netflix.

Try mapping that in your neat little funnel diagram.

The AI Advantage: Instead of forcing customers into your funnel fantasy, AI helps you understand their actual journey and meet them where they are.

THE THREE FUNNEL FAILURES THAT KILL CONVERSIONS

Failure 1: The Assumption Avalanche

When I was distributing Dirtsurfers all across the US, our funnel assumed people would:

- See product → Get excited → Research specs → Buy
- Reality: See product → Feel confused → Wonder about injury risk → Google "Dirtsurfer crashes" → Leave forever

We were solving for excitement when we should've been solving for fear and confusion.

The AI Fix: Assembly AI team discovered their real funnel problem. They fed 1,000+ customer support tickets into AI with a prompt similar to this:

"Act as a behavioral conversion strategist who specializes in analyzing pre-purchase customer sentiment and decision-making.

I'll paste below real support tickets, chat logs, or inquiry emails from potential customers of our [product/service]. These are people considering an online course or program.

Please analyze the text for:

1. Questions they asked BEFORE purchasing
2. Clues about their emotional state or mindset when they reached out
3. The moment (or information) that finally pushed them to buy
4. Obstacles, hesitations, or sticking points that nearly stopped them

Then:

- Summarize patterns you notice across multiple cases
- Identify key trust gaps and misconceptions prospects may have about online programs like ours
- Suggest messaging angles or micro-copy ideas that could build trust earlier (e.g. testimonials, clarity, risk reversal, etc.)"

The revelation? Price wasn't the issue. Trust was.

New funnel focus: Proof before pitch. They provided transparency, proof, and testimonials.

Result: First response time was reduced 97%, Resolution rate increased from 25% to 50%, and customer satisfaction scores increased by 15-25% within the first few months.[1]

Failure 2: The One-Size-Fits-None Nightmare

Your small business customers and enterprise clients don't buy the same way. Yet most funnels treat them identically.

The Chooch.ai Transformation

This AI computer vision company had a classic complex B2B problem:

- Long, technical sales cycles
- Multiple decision makers

- Buyers at different sophistication levels
- A generic funnel trying to serve everyone

They partnered with Growth Hackers to implement AI-driven funnel intelligence:

Lead Scoring Revolution: AI analyzed thousands of data points to identify which prospects were actually ready to buy vs. just researching.

Dynamic Content Delivery: Different messages for CTOs (technical specs) vs. CFOs (ROI data) vs. end users (ease of use).

Behavioral Triggering: AI monitored specific actions (such as downloading certain resources or visiting pricing multiple times) and triggered relevant follow-ups.

The results:

- Manual lead qualification time: Down 70%
- Sales team focus: Only high-intent prospects
- Revenue outcome: $20M Series A funding

That's not just a better funnel. That's a fundamentally different way of selling.[2]

Failure 3: The Set-and-Forget Fantasy

Building a funnel and walking away is like planting a garden and never watering it. Yet that's exactly what most businesses do.

The Living Funnel Approach

Here's what AI enables: funnels that evolve based on what's actually working.

Real example from DealHub, a B2B software company facing the same challenge I see everywhere: driving traffic is easy, but converting it is hard. Their standard funnel was: whitepaper download → email nurture → sales call. It was delivering modest results at maybe 1-2%

conversion. Respectable, but not remarkable. They knew something had to change.

The Transformation Timeline:

Starting Point: Traditional B2B funnel with typical conversion rates.

First AI Discovery: By implementing 6sense's AI analytics, DealHub uncovered a pattern hiding in plain sight—prospects who engaged with case studies and customer proof points converted at dramatically higher rates. Not marginally better. Dramatically better.

Nobody had noticed because they were too focused on top-of-funnel metrics.

The Adjustment: Case studies have moved from being buried resources to prominent positions in the buyer's journey, especially just before sales calls.

Second AI Insight: The system detected another correlation. Video content is a conversion predictor. Customer testimonials and product walkthroughs weren't just nice-to-have; they were purchase indicators.

The Response: Video testimonials landed on high-intent pages and key nurture emails.

Full AI Optimization: Through continuous analysis, DealHub refined every stage of the funnel. AI surfaced the right content at the right time, personalized outreach based on engagement, and helped sales focus on the hottest accounts.

The Results:

- Lead quality improved 10x (they stopped chasing everyone, started converting the right ones)
- Inbound traffic up 55%
- Conversion rates saw significant lifts across all stages
- Most importantly, they could finally tie marketing activity directly to revenue

Same basic funnel structure. Completely different results.

The lesson? Your funnel has hidden patterns that predict success. AI identifies them, tests them, and continually compounds improvements. While your competitors run the same playbook from five years ago, you're evolving every month based on what actually works.[3]

Building Your AI-Enhanced Funnel Architecture

Forget everything you learned about funnel stages. Here's the framework that actually works:

THE M.A.P. SYSTEM (MOMENTS, ACTIONS, PATHWAYS)

Moments: Critical decision points where prospects either advance or abandon.

Actions: Specific behaviors that signal intent or concern.

Pathways: Customized routes based on prospect behavior.

Here's how to build it:

Step 1: Moment Mapping with AI

Prompt for ChatGPT/Claude: "I sell [product/service] to [target audience]. Based on common buyer psychology, what are the 5 critical moments where prospects decide to:

1. Keep learning more.
2. Abandon their research. Include the emotional state and key questions at each moment."

Step 2: Action Intelligence

Feed your analytics into AI: "Here's behavioral data from our website: [Paste Google Analytics behavior flow]

Identify:

1. Actions that correlate with purchase
2. Actions that predict abandonment
3. Unusual patterns worth testing"

Step 3: Pathway Personalization

This is where magic happens. Instead of one funnel, you create intelligent pathways:

For the Skeptic Path: Heavy on proof, testimonials, guarantees.

For the Analyst Path: Data, specs, ROI calculators.

For the Innovator Path: Focus on what's new and different.

For the Consensus Builder: Easy-to-share resources, team pricing

AI helps identify which visitors fit which path based on their behavior.

Your Funnel Audit Checklist

Before building new, audit what you have:

Traffic Reality Check

- Where do visitors actually come from? (Not where you think)
- What's their intent level? (Browsing vs. buying)
- What questions are they trying to answer?

Conversion Forensics

- Where exactly do people leave?
- What's the last thing they see before leaving?
- What content do converters consume that abandoners don't?

Message-Market Fit

- Does each stage answer the visitor's current question?
- Are you pushing for the sale before building trust?
- Do different segments see different messages?

I use this prompt for quick audits:

"Analyze this funnel flow: [Stage 1]: [Page/Content] [Stage 2]: [Page/Content] [etc]

For someone who [describe their situation], identify:

1. Gaps in logic or trust
2. Missing information they'd need
3. Reasons they might abandon at each stage"

The Offer Architecture That Actually Converts

Here's a painful truth: Most lead magnets suck. "10 Tips for..." PDFs that nobody reads. "Ultimate Guides" that aren't ultimate or guiding.

Your offer needs to be so valuable that your prospect would feel stupid NOT taking it.

The S.O.L.V.E. Framework

Specific problem it addresses
Outcome they'll achieve
Limited time to get results
Valuable enough to pay for
Easy to implement immediately

Example transformation:

Before: "Free Marketing Guide for Small Businesses" (Generic, vague, probably useless)

After: "The 15-Minute Market Research Template That Revealed $2.3M in Hidden Revenue" (Specific, outcome-focused, time-bound, proven value)

AI-Powered Offer Development

Experiment with this prompt:

"My audience is [specific description]. Their biggest pain point is [specific problem]. They've tried [common solutions] but struggled because of [reasons].

Create 10 lead magnet ideas that:

1. Solve one specific aspect of their problem
2. Deliver results in under [timeframe]
3. Require no special tools or knowledge
4. Sound too valuable to be free
5. Lead naturally to my paid offer: [description]"

Industry Leaders Show What's Possible

These companies aren't just using AI to tweak their funnels; they're reimagining how funnels work:

Capgemini + Aptivio: 40% increase in sales-ready opportunities by using AI to identify genuine buyer intent (not just engagement).[4]

ACI Corporation + Salesken: Real-time AI coaching during sales calls, personalizing the funnel conversation-by-conversation.[5]

Adstra's Results:

- 209 qualified calls in 46 days
- $142K revenue from $26K spend in 30 days
- How? AI-driven funnel optimization that adapted hourly

The pattern is clear: Static funnels are dead. Intelligent, adaptive pathways are the future.[6]

YOUR 14-DAY FUNNEL TRANSFORMATION PLAN

Days 1-3: The Forensic Audit

- Map your current funnel (even if it's ugly)
- Identify the top 3 leak points
- Collect all customer questions/objections

Days 4-6: The AI Deep Dive

- Feed data into AI for analysis
- Generate pathway hypotheses
- Create behavioral trigger maps

Days 7-10: The Minimum Viable Test

- Pick ONE pathway to optimize
- Implement 3-5 specific improvements
- Set up proper tracking

Days 11-14: The Learning Loop

- Analyze results
- Feed findings back to AI
- Plan next iteration

Don't try to fix everything at once. Fix one pathway, prove it works, then expand.

The Psychology of Funnel Optimization

Here's what took me years to understand: Funnels aren't about pushing people forward. They're about removing reasons to go backward.

At every stage of your funnel, prospects are asking:

- "Is this for someone like me?"
- "Can I trust these people?"
- "Will this actually work?"
- "What if I'm making a mistake?"

Miss one question, lose the sale.

The Trust Acceleration Formula

At SalesHive, managing 100 cold callers taught me a crucial lesson: the speed of trust determines the speed of qualified appointments.

Here's how AI helps build trust faster:

Micro-Commitments: AI identifies the smallest possible "yes" at each stage

Social Proof Timing: Delivers testimonials at the exact moment of doubt.

Risk Reversal: Addresses specific fears based on behavior patterns.

Authority Signals: Reinforces credibility when skepticism peaks.

Real example: HubSpot noticed that prospects who watched customer story videos converted five times better. AI now detects hesitation behaviors (such as return visits and prolonged page dwell times) and automatically surfaces relevant video testimonials. Conversion rate increase: 73%. [7]

THE HIDDEN FUNNEL KILLERS NOBODY TALKS ABOUT

Killer 1: The Curse of Knowledge

You know your product inside out. Your prospects don't. What seems obvious to you is Greek to them.

I learned this brutally with Dirtsurfer. We kept talking about "fluid, arcing turns" and "gyroscopic effects." Our customers just wanted to know: "Will I die?"

The AI Solution: Feed your funnel copy into ChatGPT with this prompt:

"Pretend you know nothing about [industry/product]. Read this copy and list:

1. Terms that need explanation
2. Assumptions made about prior knowledge

3. Simpler ways to say the same thing"

Killer 2: The Mobile Maze

If 67% of your funnel traffic is mobile, then is 67% of your funnel designed for thumbs?

Quick Mobile Audit:

- Can you complete your funnel one-handed?
- Are forms painful on phone keyboards?
- Do pop-ups make mobile visitors rage-quit?

AI tools like Hotjar's AI insights can analyze mobile behavior and identify exactly where phone users abandon ship.

Killer 3: The Speed Trap

Every second of load time costs conversions. But here's the kicker: Perceived speed matters more than actual speed.

The Perception Hack: AI can help prioritize what loads first. That hero image? Load text first so visitors can start reading while images appear.

ADVANCED FUNNEL STRATEGIES THAT FEEL LIKE CHEATING

Strategy 1: The Invisible Retargeting Funnel

Instead of hammering abandoners with "Come back!" ads, build an invisible education funnel:

1. They abandon at the pricing page
2. Retargeting shows a case study ad (not a sales pitch)
3. The case study includes ROI data
4. A natural link back to pricing with new context

Retargeting conversions jumped 240%.

Strategy 2: The Trojan Horse Funnel

Sometimes the best funnel doesn't look like a funnel.

Example: SmartAsset, an accounting software company, created a "Tax Savings Calculator."

- No email required
- Genuinely useful tool
- The results page naturally mentions their software
- Their optional "Save my calculation" requires an email

Lead quality: 10 times better than ebook downloads.[8]

Strategy 3: The Choose-Your-Adventure Funnel

Let prospects control their journey: "I want to see: A) ROI data and case studies. B) Product demo and features. C) Pricing and packages"

AI personalizes everything that comes after based on their choice. Self-segmentation beats any algorithm.

Measuring What Actually Matters

Forget vanity metrics. Here's what actually predicts funnel success:

Speed to Value: How quickly do they experience a win?

Engagement Depth: Better to have 100 people watch your entire demo than 1,000 who bounce after 10 seconds

Question Quality: Support questions shifting from "What is this?" to "How do I maximize this?" = winning

Referral Triggers: When do customers become advocates?

Use this AI prompt monthly:

"Analyze these funnel metrics: [Paste your data]

Identify:

1. Leading indicators of conversion
2. Hidden correlations
3. Optimization opportunities ranked by impact"

THE FUNNEL TRANSFORMATION STORIES

The Wedding Venue Wonder

Remember my $72K wedding venue success? Here's the funnel that made it happen:

Old Funnel: Beautiful photos → Tour request → Price shock → Ghost

New Funnel (after analysis): Recently engaged women focused ad → $2,000 value lead magnet → "Book by Feb 14th" CTA → Virtual tour with pricing context → Booking

The key insight: We weren't selling to local brides with a $1,000 budget. We were selling to metropolitan women with a $30,000 budget who wanted the "Old South" fantasy wedding.

The Dental Practice Pivot

That emergency dental practice I mentioned? Their funnel transformation:

Before: Generic "Book Appointment" button everywhere.

After:

- Homepage: "Dental Emergency? Get Seen in 2 Hours"
- Quiz: "Is This a Dental Emergency?" (educational, not scary)
- Booking page: Shows real-time availability
- Confirmation: What to expect, what to bring

Emergency bookings up 67%. Why? The funnel matched their mental state: panic → relief → trust → booking.[9]

Your Funnel Optimization Commandments

1. **Test Big Swings, Not Tiny Tweaks**: Button color changes aren't transformational. Instead, test completely different approaches.
2. **Speed Beats Perfection**: Launch ugly funnels fast, then optimize based on real data.
3. **Behavior Beats Demographics**: What they do matters more than who they are.
4. **Questions Beat Statements**: "Struggling with X?" beats "We solve X"
5. **Progress Beats Perfection**: Show them how far they've come, not how far they have to go.

The One Funnel Question That Changes Everything

Before you build or optimize anything, answer this: "What's the one belief they need to have before they'll buy?"

For Dirtsurfer, it was "This is safe enough to try." For the wedding venue, it was "This is worth the investment." For the dental practice, it was "I can get help right now."

Everything in your funnel should build toward that one belief.

COMMON FUNNEL MISTAKES (SO YOU CAN AVOID MY PAIN)

Mistake 1: Optimizing a Fundamentally Broken Funnel

Like putting premium gas in a car with no engine. If your core offer sucks, no amount of funnel optimization will save you.

Mistake 2: Following "Best Practices" Blindly

What works for SaaS might kill e-commerce. What works for B2B might confuse B2C. Test everything.

Mistake 3: Ignoring the Messy Middle

Most funnels focus on the top (acquisition) and the bottom (conversion). The middle, where trust is built, is often overlooked. That's where AI shines, identifying exactly what builds or breaks trust.

Your Next Steps

1. **Run the audit prompts** on your current funnel
2. **Pick ONE pathway** to optimize first
3. **Set up proper tracking** (you can't improve what you don't measure)
4. **Start with mobile** (most significant impact for most)
5. **Feed results back to AI** for continuous improvement

Remember: Your funnel is never "done." It's a living system that should evolve with every visitor.

Coming up: You've got positioning that resonates and a funnel that converts. But what do you fill it with? Chapter 4 reveals how AI transforms content creation from a major bottleneck into a competitive advantage.

CHAPTER 4
TRANSFORMING CONTENT CREATION WITH AI TOOLS

TUESDAY, 9:47 PM. You're staring at a blank Google Doc, cursor blinking mockingly. The client needs five blog posts by Friday. You've written three sentences in the past hour, deleted them all, and are now seriously considering a career in professional dog walking. Sound familiar?

That was me, three years ago, before I discovered what AI could really do for content ideation. Not the "write generic garbage" AI everyone warns about, but AI as a creative partner that helps you produce more authentic content than ever before.

When you start using AI correctly, that same client can get 20 pieces of content in just a few hours. And here's the kicker, it sounds more authentic than when you were agonizing over every word.

THE CONTENT CRISIS NOBODY WANTS TO ADMIT

Let's get real about content marketing in 2025 and beyond:

- Everyone says, "Content is King."
- Everyone's drowning in content demands
- Most content is vanilla, bland, forgettable, and pointless

At Smart Business Development, we once had a client who insisted on blogging daily. After six months of grinding out posts about "5 Ways to Improve Your Business" and "Why Customer Service Matters," their traffic had actually decreased.

Why? Because nobody needs another mediocre blog post. What they need is content that actually helps them solve real problems.

WHY MOST AI CONTENT FAILS (AND HOW TO FIX IT)

Here's the dirty secret about AI content: It's not the AI that sucks, it's how you're using it.

Failure Mode 1: The Robot Regurgitation

What everyone does: "Write a blog post about email marketing tips."

What AI produces: "In today's digital landscape, email marketing remains a crucial component of any comprehensive marketing strategy..."

Barf!

The fix: Stop asking AI to write for you. Start asking it to brainstorm with you.

Better prompt: "I run a small law firm. My clients are stressed-out business owners who are being sued. They're too busy to read long emails but need to stay informed about their case. What unconventional email strategies could help me communicate effectively with them?"

See the difference? Context. Specificity. Real problems.

Failure Mode 2: The Prompt-and-Pray

Most people treat AI like a Magic 8-Ball. Shake it (prompt it) and hope for the best.

That's like hiring an employee, giving them zero training, then wondering why they underperform.

The Partnership Approach:

When I create content now, it's a conversation:

1. I feed AI context about my audience
2. We brainstorm angles together
3. I guide the structure
4. AI helps with first drafts
5. I inject stories and personality
6. AI helps polish and optimize

It's not AI replacing me. It's AI amplifying me.

Failure Mode 3: The Consistency Catastrophe

Three different people using AI = three different brand voices. Chaos.

At SalesHive, managing 100 cold-callers taught me a crucial lesson: Scripts only work when everyone sounds authentic within the same framework.

The Voice Framework Solution:

Create a "voice bank" for your AI:

- 10 examples of your best content
- List of phrases you love/hate
- Stories and analogies you often use
- Your unique perspective on common topics

Feed this to the AI before creating any content. Now it writes in your voice, not generic AI-speak.

THE CONTENT CALENDAR THAT RUNS ITSELF

Remember when I mentioned spending Sunday nights planning content? That special hell is optional now.

The Old Way vs. The AI Way

Old Way:

- Stare at a blank calendar
- Panic about ideas
- Copy what competitors are doing
- Batch create in exhausting marathons
- Burn out by month three

AI Way:

- Feed AI your business goals and audience insights
- Generate 90 days of strategic content ideas in 20 minutes
- Each idea connects to business objectives
- Create content in focused 30-minute sprints
- Actually enjoy the process

Try this content calendar prompt:

"You are a highly effective content marketing professional. Help me plan content for [business description].

Target audience: [detailed description] Business goals this quarter: [specific objectives] Competitors are talking about: [themes to differentiate from] Our unique angles: [what makes us different]

Create a 30-day content calendar with:

- 3 pillar topics (major themes)
- 2 posts per week per pillar
- A mix of content types (educational, story-based, actionable)
- Natural progression building toward [specific CTA]
- Titles that would make someone stop scrolling

Avoid: Generic advice, corporate speak, and topics everyone covers."

In just minutes, you have a month of strategic content mapped out.

THE ASSET CREATION REVOLUTION

Now for the fun part, actually creating content that doesn't suck.

The S.T.O.R.Y. Framework

Every piece of content needs:

Situation - What problem are we solving?

Tension - Why does it matter right now?

Observation - What insight do we offer?

Resolution - How do we solve it?

You - What should they do next?

This works for blog posts, emails, social media posts, and even video scripts.

Real example:

Situation: Small business owner spending 10 hours/week on social media **Tension**: Competition posting daily is making him feel left behind

Observation: Quality beats quantity if you know what resonates **Resolution**: Use AI to test 20 variations, find what works, and double down

You: Download our "AI Content Testing Template."

350% more engagement than their previous posts.

The Multi-Format Magic Trick

Here's where AI becomes your content multiplication machine.

Start with ONE core piece. Let's say it's a blog post about customer retention. Now transform it:

The Multiplication Prompt:

"Take this blog post about [topic] and transform it into:

1. 5 tweets with different angles
2. LinkedIn post focusing on my personal story
3. Email newsletter with actionable tips
4. Instagram carousel breaking down key points
5. 30-second video script
6. Podcast talking points
7. One-page PDF checklist

Maintain the core message but adapt tone and format for each platform."

One hour of work becomes a week of content.

VMWARE'S CONTENT TRANSFORMATION STORY

Let me share a story that proves this isn't just theory.

VMware, no longer a scrappy startup, was drowning in content demands:

- Product launches needed supporting content
- Multiple teams creating inconsistent materials
- Quality varying wildly across pieces
- Editors overwhelmed with basic fixes

They implemented Acrolinx, an AI content governance platform.

Results:

- 73% of users reported quality improvements
- 60% became more efficient creators
- Editors freed from grunt work to focus on strategy
- Consistent brand voice across thousands of pieces

The lesson? AI doesn't replace human creativity. It eliminates the friction that prevents creativity from flowing. [1]

THE INDUSTRY LEADERS' PLAYBOOK

Here's how the big players are using AI for content domination:

Ingersoll Rand: Uses AI to create dynamic content based on real-time data (weather affecting HVAC needs). Your version? Use AI to create timely content based on trends in your industry. [2]

SteelSync Solutions: Delivers hyper-personalized content to B2B buyers. Your approach? Use AI to segment your list and create variations for each segment.[3]

Tely AI's Client Results:

- 1,990 to 17,500 organic clicks in 6 months
- 199K to 2.03M impressions
- Minimal human input

The pattern? AI handles volume and optimization. Humans handle strategy and authenticity.[4]

YOUR CONTENT CREATION TOOLKIT

Try this setup for content that converts:

For Writing:

Primary - Claude for long-form (better at maintaining context)

Secondary - ChatGPT for ideation and variations

Specialty - Jasper for marketing-specific templates

For Design:

Canva Magic Write - Creates on-brand visuals with integrated copy

Lumen5 - Transforms blog posts into videos

DALL-E - Custom images that don't look like stock photos

For Distribution:

Buffer/Publer - Schedule across platforms

Make.com - Automate the entire publishing workflow

Opus Clip - Turn long videos into social clips

Total cost: Under $200 per month. Results: Priceless.

The Content Quality Checklist

Before publishing anything, run it through this filter:

The H.E.L.P. Test:

- **H**elpful: Does it solve a real problem?
- **E**ngaging: Would you read it if you didn't write it?
- **L**egitimate: Is it accurate and honest?
- **P**urposeful: Does it move readers toward a goal?

If it fails any test, go back to the drawing board.

COMMON CONTENT CREATION PITFALLS

Pitfall 1: The SEO Zombie Trap

Creating content for algorithms instead of humans. Yes, keywords matter. No, they shouldn't drive everything.

Fix: Write for humans first, then optimize for search.

Pitfall 2: The Perfection Paralysis

That blog post you've been "polishing" for three weeks? Ship it. Perfect content that never publishes helps nobody.

Fix: Set time limits, with a maximum of 2 hours for a blog post. Done is better than perfect.

Pitfall 3: The Ego Edit

Rejecting AI suggestions because "I'm the writer here."

Fix: Remember, AI is your intern, not your replacement. Use what helps and ignore what doesn't.

THE STRATEGIC CONTENT PLAYS NOBODY'S TALKING ABOUT

Play 1: The Trojan Horse Series

Create genuinely helpful content that naturally leads to your solution. Example: Dental practice created "5-Minute Morning Routines for Healthier Teeth." Positions them as caring about prevention, not just treatment. New patient inquiries rose 40%.[5]

Play 2: The Reality Show Approach

Document your process; don't just share results.I started sharing my AI content experiments, failures included. Engagement tripled. People trust transparency.

Play 3: The Remix Revolution

Take your competitors' top-performing content and create the opposite angle. They say "10 Best Practices"? You create "10 Best Practices That Actually Hurt Your Business."

YOUR 7-DAY CONTENT SPRINT

Monday: Audit your last 10 pieces. What performed? What flopped? Why?

Tuesday: Create your voice bank. Feed it to AI.

Wednesday: Generate a 30-day calendar using the prompt above.

Thursday: Batch create 5 pieces using the S.T.O.R.Y. framework.

Friday: Transform each piece into 3 different formats.

Weekend: Schedule everything. Take actual time off.

Following Monday: Analyze performance. Feed insights back to AI. Iterate.

THE MINDSET SHIFT THAT CHANGES EVERYTHING

Stop thinking of content as something you "have to" create. Start thinking of it as conversations you "get to" have.

Every piece of content is a chance to help someone solve a problem you've already figured out. AI enables you to have more of those conversations faster without burning out.

At Dirtsurfer, our best content came from our customers. Riders loved shooting videos on themselves having fun on our product. It created social proof, answering real customer fears. "Is it hard to ride and how do I stop so I don't get hurt?"

Your audience has questions. You have answers. AI helps you bridge that gap at scale.

The Content Reality Check

Before moving on, ask yourself:

- What's the one piece of content you've been procrastinating on?
- What if you could create it in 30 minutes instead of 3 hours?
- What would you do with all that reclaimed time?

That's not a hypothetical. That's your new reality with AI.

Coming up: You've got killer content, but where should it live? Chapter 5 reveals how AI takes the guesswork out of channel selection and builds distribution systems that work.

CHAPTER 5

WINNING THE CHANNEL GAME WITH AI STRATEGY

"WE NEED TO BE ON TIKTOK!"

The CEO's declaration hit the conference room like a grenade. Their B2B manufacturing client, with an average customer age of 52, wanted to dance on TikTok because their competitor had gone viral with a forklift safety video.

I've heard stories like this a hundred times. Replace TikTok with Clubhouse, Pinterest, BeReal, or whatever platform is hot this week. The fear of missing out (FOMO) is real, and it's draining marketing budgets everywhere.

Here's what I learned the hard way at Dirtsurfer: Being on the wrong channels is worse than being on no channels. We spent months trying to infiltrate skateboarding forums. You know what we got? Banned, mocked, and exactly zero sales.

Our real customers? They were reading "Outside Magazine" and hanging out in adventure travel forums. One channel switch changed everything.

THE CHANNEL SELECTION MATRIX NOBODY TEACHES YOU

Forget the "be everywhere" advice. Here's the truth: You can dominate 2 to 3 channels or be mediocre on 10. I know which one pays the bills.

The Channel Reality Check

Before you chase the next shiny platform, answer these:

1. **Where does your audience go to solve problems?** (Not just hang out)
2. **What mindset are they in on each platform?** (LinkedIn = professional, Instagram = aspirational)
3. **Can you commit to showing up consistently?** (Abandoned channels scream "failing business")
4. **Does the platform's strength align with your content type?** (Dancing manufacturers, anyone?)

Most businesses can't answer those questions. They're guessing. AI eliminates the guesswork.

THE SPARKTORO REVELATION

Beerwulf, a digital craft beer platform launched by Heineken, claimed its audience lived on Instagram. "Millennials love craft beer and Instagram!" they insisted.

Twenty minutes with SparkToro revealed the truth:

- Their actual customers followed beer rating apps, not influencers
- They read brewing blogs, not lifestyle content
- They hung out in Reddit's homebrew communities
- Instagram was their 7th most-used platform

The marketing team shifted the budget from Instagram influencers to Reddit community engagement and partnerships with beer apps. Sales from marketing grew 4x in 90 days. That's the power of data over assumptions.[1]

THE THREE CHANNEL CATEGORIES THAT MATTER

After analyzing hundreds of campaigns, I've found every effective channel strategy includes three types:

1. The Authority Builder - Where you establish expertise and thought leadership.

B2B: Usually LinkedIn or industry publications

B2C: Often YouTube or niche communities

Local: Sometimes traditional media or community platforms

This isn't about selling. It's about becoming the preeminent expert.

2. The Relationship Nurturer - Where ongoing conversations happen naturally:

Email: Still the king for most businesses

SMS: For time-sensitive or local businesses

Communities: Discord, Slack, or specialized forums

These are where trust transforms into transactions.

3. The Discovery Engine - Where new people find you:

Search: SEO or PPC for intent-based businesses

Social: Platform varies by audience

Partnerships: Often overlooked, always powerful

These are your growth drivers.

Most businesses need one channel from each category. That's it.

Building Distribution Systems That Don't Break

Here's my dirty secret from the agency days: We built beautiful strategies that fell apart in execution because the tech stack was held together with digital duct tape or relied too heavily on overworked humans. Ever happen to you?

THE INTEGRATION NIGHTMARE

What usually happens:

- Tool 1 doesn't talk to Tool 2
- Manual copying between platforms
- "It worked yesterday" becomes your catchphrase
- You spend more time troubleshooting than marketing

The AI-Powered Solution:

Modern AI tools don't just create content; they orchestrate entire distribution systems.

Here is a real example from Thule Group, the outdoor gear company you've probably seen on car rooftops everywhere:

The Challenge: Thule sells products in 81 markets worldwide. They needed to:

- Post product updates across multiple channels and languages
- Personalize content for each platform and region
- Track performance globally
- Do this for tens of thousands of products weekly

The Old Way: Two full-time employees manually posting, constant errors, inconsistent messaging across markets

The AI Way: Thule implemented Productsup's AI-powered platform that transformed their entire content distribution:

1. Product data feeds into a centralized system
2. Automation monitors for any updates
3. AI generates platform-specific copy at scale
4. Visuals created and optimized automatically
5. Content is distributed across all channels

6. Analytics flow back for continuous optimization

Time investment: Adding a new channel or market now takes about 1 hour. Managing the entire system? Minimal oversight needed.

The results knocked me out:

- Manual workload practically eliminated
- Errors and inconsistencies vanished
- Product launches accelerated dramatically
- Personalized, localized marketing at scale
- Brand consistency across 81 markets

That's not just efficiency. That's a competitive moat. While competitors struggle to update content in five markets, Thule manages 81 seamlessly. Their AI-driven system scales effortlessly where human systems would collapse.[2]

The lesson? Stop thinking about AI as a content creator. Start thinking about it as your global operations manager who never sleeps, never makes mistakes, and scales infinitely.

THE SLIM CHICKENS SUCCESS STORY

Let me share a story that shows what's possible when AI meets smart channel strategy.

Slim Chickens faced a delicious problem: expanding from 100 to 300 locations meant that marketing complexity had exploded. Each location needed:

- Localized messaging
- Market-specific channel mix
- Budget optimization across platforms
- Performance tracking at scale

Their traditional agency approach was breaking down. Enter AI.

The Transformation:

Instead of one-size-fits-all campaigns, they built AI-driven local intelligence:

1. **Geo-behavioral Analysis**: AI analyzed mobile data to understand local customer patterns
2. **Dynamic Channel Selection**: Each market got its own channel mix (college towns heavy on Snapchat, suburbs focused on Facebook)
3. **Automated Localization**: National campaigns adapted automatically for local preferences
4. **Real-time Optimization**: AI shifted budgets hourly based on performance

The Results:

- 300 locations (3x growth) with the same marketing headcount
- Increased same-store sales through better targeting
- Marketing efficiency that made franchise expansion profitable

The lesson? AI doesn't just help you execute channels better. It helps you choose better channels. [2]

CHANNEL LEADERS: THE PLAYBOOK

Here's how category leaders approach channels with AI:

The Weather Company: Uses AI to analyze weather, events, and local trends to adjust channel mix in real time. Your version? Use free weather APIs + ChatGPT to adjust messaging. [3]

McDonald's: AI-powered menu boards that change based on time, weather, and local events. Your play? Dynamic email content based on customer context. [4]

The Channel Audit That Changes Everything

Before adding any channel, run this audit:

The R.O.C.K. Framework

Reach: How many of your ideal customers are actually there?

Ownership: Do you control the relationship, or does the platform?

Cost: Include time, not just money

Knowledge: Can you realistically excel here?

Score each channel 1-10 on each factor. Anything under 25 total? Skip it.

The AI Channel Intelligence Prompt - Here's my go-to for channel analysis:

"I run a [business type] serving [target audience]. My customers [describe their behavior and preferences]. My competitors are active on [list channels].

Analyze:

1. Where my specific audience is most likely to make purchase decisions
2. Which channels align with my content strengths
3. Gaps in competitor channel strategies I could exploit
4. The optimal channel mix for my resources

Consider both digital and traditional channels."

ADVANCED CHANNEL STRATEGIES

Strategy 1: The Channel Arbitrage Play

Find overpriced attention on one channel, underpriced on another.

Example: B2B software company discovered:

- LinkedIn ads: $12 per click
- Industry newsletter sponsorships: $0.80 per click
- Same audience quality

Shifted 70% of budget: same leads, 85% less cost.

Strategy 2: The Platform Jujitsu Method

Use platform strengths against competitors stuck in old patterns.

Kenney Property Services noticed that all its competitors used stock photos. They created before/after TikToks of actual jobs. Authentic content on a "young" platform reached homeowners tired of generic ads. New customer acquisition costs dropped by 60%. [5]

Strategy 3: The Dark Social Strategy

Most attribution misses "dark social," private shares, direct messages (DMs), and word-of-mouth referrals.

Solution: Create content designed to be shared privately.

- Calculators people share with spouses
- "Is this normal?" quizzes people DM to friends
- Industry inside jokes for Slack channels

A law firm tracked its "Is my business partner screwing me?" quiz. Official shares: 47. Estimated private shares: 2,000+.[6]

CHANNEL-SPECIFIC AI OPTIMIZATION

Email: The Sleeping Giant

Everyone says email is dead. Everyone is wrong.

AI Email Superpowers:

- Send time optimization (when each person actually opens)
- Subject line testing at scale

- Content personalization beyond "Hi [Name]"
- Re-engagement campaigns that actually work

Prompt for better email: "Rewrite this email for someone who:

- Opened our last 3 emails but didn't click
- Visited our pricing page 2 weeks ago
- Works in [industry] with [title]
- Make it feel personal, not creepy."

LINKEDIN: THE B2B GOLDMINE

AI LinkedIn Tactics:

- Analyze viral posts in your niche for patterns
- Generate authentic-sounding thought leadership
- Optimize posting times by engagement data
- Create response templates that start conversations

The 3-2-1 Formula:

- 3 valuable insights
- 2 personal observations
- 1 question to drive engagement

PAID CHANNELS: THE MONEY MULTIPLIER

AI + Paid = Profit:

- Creative testing at a massive scale
- Micro-audience targeting
- Bid optimization by actual value, not just clicks
- Cross-channel attribution modeling

We helped a church client test 50 ad variations in a week. Cost per acquisition dropped 73%. Human creativity + AI scale = unstoppable.

YOUR CHANNEL IMPLEMENTATION ROADMAP

Week 1: The Reality Audit

- List current channels and actual time investment
- Run the R.O.C.K. analysis
- Use SparkToro or similar for audience intelligence

Week 2: The Strategic Pruning

- Cut the bottom 50% of channels (yes, really)
- Reinvest time in top performers
- Set up basic automation for survivors

Week 3: The AI Enhancement

- Implement one AI tool per remaining channel
- Create templates and workflows
- Establish measurement systems

Week 4: The Optimization Loop

- Analyze performance data
- Feed insights to AI for recommendations
- Plan next month's experiments

CHANNEL MISTAKES THAT COST MONEY

Mistake 1: The Shiny Object Syndrome

Chasing new platforms before mastering current ones.

Fix: No new channels until the current ones are 80% optimized.

Mistake 2: The Set-and-Forget Fantasy

Automation doesn't mean abandonment.

Fix: Weekly channel reviews and monthly strategy adjustments.

Mistake 3: The Vanity Metrics Trap

10,000 followers who never buy < 100 customers who love you.

Fix: Track revenue per channel, not just engagement.

The Channel Truth Nobody Admits

Here's what took me 20 years to learn: The best channel is the one you'll actually use consistently.

I don't care if TikTok is "the future" if you hate making videos. LinkedIn's ROI means nothing if writing bores you to tears. Email marketing can't save you if you ghost your list for months.

Pick channels that match your strengths, not your aspirations.

Your Channel Challenge

Before reading the next chapter, do this:

1. List every channel you're currently using
2. Calculate actual ROI (time + money) for each
3. Be honest: Which ones are you keeping out of fear?

Now, imagine cutting the bottom half and doubling down on what works. That's not giving up. That's focusing on winning.

Coming up: You've chosen your channels wisely. Now, let's fill them with leads that actually convert. Chapter 6 reveals the AI-powered lead generation systems that transform cold traffic into eager buyers.

CHAPTER 6

AUTOMATING SUCCESS: THE AI LEAD GENERATION REVOLUTION

IMAGINE THIS IS YOU..."the notification hits at 6:43 AM: "New lead assigned."

You roll over, grab your phone, and check the details. A software company with 50-200 employees downloaded your "Marketing Automation Buyer's Guide," visited your pricing page three times, and engaged with four emails. Lead score: 94/100.

By the time you get to your desk with a coffee, the AI has already sent a personalized follow-up email, scheduled a calendar invite for a demo, and briefed you on their likely pain points.

That lead closes two weeks later with a $47,000 contract.

That scenario is the reality of AI-powered lead generation. Not the "spray and pray" of old-school tactics, but surgical precision that makes every conversation count.

THE LEAD GENERATION LIE WE NEED TO ADDRESS

Everyone wants "more leads." But here's what my years at SalesHive taught me: most businesses are drowning in leads. They're starving for *conversations with the right people*.

I watched as our best cold callers booked appointments while the average ones chased ghosts. The difference? They qualified ruthlessly before dialing.

AI does that qualification at scale, automatically, 24/7.

THE MATHEMATICS OF MODERN LEAD GEN

Traditional approach:

- 1,000 cold emails → 30 responses → 10 meetings → 1 sale
- Success rate: 0.1%
- Human hours: 40+
- Morale: Crushed

AI-enhanced approach:

- 1,000 targeted contacts → AI qualifies 100 high-intent → 30 personalized outreaches → 15 meetings → 3 sales
- Success rate: 0.3% (3x improvement)
- Human hours: 10
- Morale: Energized

Same list size with triple the results at a quarter of the effort.

THE THREE PILLARS OF AI LEAD GENERATION

Pillar 1: Capture Systems That Convert

Your landing page is where interest transforms into information. Most are where interest goes to die.

The Unbounce Revelation

Zola, the wedding planning platform, faced a problem every growing company knows: their landing pages were underperforming against industry benchmarks. Building new variations was painfully slow and resource-intensive. Sound familiar?

They turned to Unbounce's AI tools, and what happened next changed my entire perspective on landing page optimization:

- **Smart Copy** analyzed top-performing pages in the wedding industry
- Generated headline variations based on psychological triggers (no fake countdown timers needed)
- Created personalized messages based on traffic source
- Built page variants in hours, not weeks

The results? Zola's conversion rates jumped to between 5% and 20% across their new landing pages—crushing the industry average of 2.35%.

But here's what really blew me away: They created over 300 landing page variations in the time it used to take them to build just one. Three hundred. Each tailored to specific audiences and traffic sources.

The highest-performing elements didn't just stay on landing pages, they rolled them out to their main homepage, amplifying the impact across their entire digital presence.

That's not just better copywriting. That's a fundamental shift in how landing pages get built, tested, and optimized. [1]

THE CONVERSION PSYCHOLOGY AI UNDERSTANDS (THAT WE OFTEN FORGET)

People don't convert on features. They convert on futures, the future they'll have after solving their problem.

My favorite landing page prompt: "You are an expert at designing high-converting landing pages. Create landing page copy for [product/service].

Visitor context: They've just [specific action that brought them here]

Their current pain: [specific struggle]

Their desired outcome: [what success looks like]

Write:

1. Headline that mirrors their internal dialogue
2. Subheadline that hints at the solution
3. 3 bullet points of transformation (not features)
4. CTA that feels like the logical next step

Avoid: Hype, pressure tactics, generic benefits."

Feel free to steal that prompt and test it out for yourself.

Pillar 2: Nurture Sequences That Sell

Here's where most lead gen fails: The follow-up. You capture a lead, send one "Thanks for downloading!" email, and then blast them with newsletters until they unsubscribe. That's not nurturing. That's negligence.

The Lemos Coaching Transformation

They were drowning in manual follow-up. Every lead got the same generic sequence. Conversion rate: 2%.

They turned to an AI-powered nurture system:

1. **Behavioral Triggers**: AI watched what leads did (or didn't do)
2. **Dynamic Pathing**: Different sequences for different actions
3. **Personalized Outreach**: Each email referenced their specific situation
4. **Smart Timing**: Messages sent when engagement was highest

The sequence that changed everything:

Email 1 (Immediate): Deliver value, ask one question

Email 2 (Day 2): Answer to yesterday's question + case study

Email 3 (Day 4): Address specific objections based on their industry

Email 4 (Day 7): Invitation to private training

Email 5 (Day 10): Success story + soft pitch

Email 6 (Day 14): Break-up email with genuine value

The conversion rate jumped to 82%. Same leads. Different approach. [2]

Pillar 3: Intelligent Lead Scoring

Not all leads are created equal. AI knows the difference.

Traditional scoring: Downloaded ebook = 10 points. Visited pricing = 20 points. **Problem**: A student who's researching and a CEO who's buying will score the same.

AI scoring considers:

- Behavioral patterns over time
- Company signals (hiring, funding, technology stack)
- Engagement quality, not just quantity
- Comparison to similar customers who converted

The Technology Stack That Delivers

Here's an effective setup for AI-powered lead generation:

For Landing Pages:

- **Unbounce or Leadpages**: AI-powered builders
- **Swipe Pages**: When you need speed over customization
- **Carrd**: For simple, fast-loading pages

For Email Automation:

- **MailerLite**: Best AI features for the price
- **ConvertKit**: Creator-focused with smart automation
- **ActiveCampaign**: When you need serious firepower

For Lead Intelligence:

- **Clearbit or Apollo**: Company and contact enrichment
- **Clay**: Spreadsheets on steroids for lead research
- **6sense or Leadfeeder**: See who's visiting before they convert

For Workflow Automation:

- **Make.com**: Visual automation for non-coders
- **n8n**: Open-source power for technical teams
- **Zapier**: When you need every integration

Total cost: $200-$500 per month, depending on the scale. ROI: Often 1000%+.

INDUSTRY LEADERS SHOW THE WAY

Leadzen.ai's Approach: AI agents making personalized calls at scale. Not robocalls, actual conversations that sound human because AI briefs them in real-time. [3]

Seamless.AI's Method: Automated contact discovery that would take humans weeks. One client identified 10,000 qualified contacts within their Ideal Customer Profile (ICP) in just one afternoon.

HubSpot's Evolution: Their AI predicts lead score based on thousands of data points. Users report 50%+ improvement in sales productivity.

The pattern? Leaders use AI to enhance human connection, not replace it.

Advanced Lead Generation Strategies

Strategy 1: The Trojan Horse Webinar

Everyone's tired of webinars. So we stopped calling them that.

"Private Training: How [Specific Company] Achieved [Specific Result]"

Same content. 4 times the registration rate.

AI helps by:

- Personalizing invites based on company profile
- Predicting optimal time slots for attendance
- Following up based on engagement level
- Scoring leads by questions asked

Strategy 2: The Invisible Qualification

Most qualification feels like an interrogation. Your new approach:

1. Create a valuable tool (calculator, assessment, analyzer)
2. The tool requires company information to work
3. AI enriches data in the background
4. Lead gets value while we gather intelligence

It is a win-win without the awkwardness.

Strategy 3: The Competitor Conquest Play

AI monitors when companies engage with competitors:

- Job postings for tools they use
- Support complaints on social media
- Search patterns indicating research

Then, positions your solution at the perfect moment.

Ethical? Absolutely. Effective? Incredibly.

COMMON LEAD GEN MISTAKES (AND AI SOLUTIONS)

Mistake 1: Casting Too Wide

"Everyone could use our product!" No. They can't. And pretending they can wastes everyone's time.

AI Fix: Build ICPs from actual customer data, not wishful thinking.

Mistake 2: One-Size-Fits-All Messaging

Your enterprise and startup leads have different problems.

AI Fix: Dynamic content based on company size, industry, and behavior.

Mistake 3: Ignoring Intent Signals

Treating all actions equally misses buying signals.

AI Fix: Pattern recognition to identify high-intent behaviors.

The Lead Gen Metrics That Matter

Forget vanity metrics. Track:

- **Lead Velocity Rate**: Are qualified leads increasing month-over-month?
- **Time to Conversation**: How fast do you engage high-intent leads?
- **Conversation to Opportunity Rate**: Are you talking to the right people?
- **Cost Per Qualified Conversation**: Not just cost per lead

AI makes these metrics accessible to everyone, not just enterprises.

YOUR 14-DAY LEAD GEN TRANSFORMATION

Days 1-3: Audit Your Current State

- Where do leads come from now?
- What's your actual conversion rate?
- Where do leads fall off?

Days 4-7: Pick One Thing to Fix

- Usually, it's the landing page
- Or the follow-up sequence
- Or the qualification process

Days 8-10: Implement AI Solution

- Start simple
- Test with a small segment
- Measure everything

Days 11-14: Optimize and Scale

- What worked? Do more
- What failed? Find out why
- Plan next improvement

THE PSYCHOLOGICAL SHIFT REQUIRED

Here's what nobody tells you about AI lead generation: The hardest part isn't the technology. It's letting go of control.

We're trained to touch every lead, craft every message, and make every decision. AI says: "Trust the system. Focus on conversations that matter."

It's scary. It's also liberating.

The Future Is Already Here

While you're reading this, AI is:

- Identifying your next best customer
- Crafting the perfect message to reach them
- Waiting for the optimal moment to connect
- Learning from every interaction

The question isn't whether to use AI for lead generation; the question is how to use it effectively. It's whether you'll do it before your competition does.

Your Lead Gen Challenge

Before the next chapter:

1. Calculate your actual cost per qualified conversation (be honest)
2. Identify your biggest lead gen bottleneck
3. Find one AI tool that could fix it

Remember: You don't need to revolutionize everything. Fix one bottleneck, and everything flows better.

Coming up: You've got the leads. Now it's time to launch. Chapter 7 reveals how AI transforms chaotic launches into coordinated victories.

HELP A FELLOW MARKETER TRANSFORM THEIR BUSINESS

YOUR TWO MINUTES COULD CHANGE SOMEONE'S MARKETING FOREVER

"The best marketing doesn't feel like marketing. It feels like helping."

TOM FISHBURNE

You know that feeling when you discover something that completely changes how you work? That's what happened to me with AI marketing tools. Now, I want to help others find that same break-through.

Would you help a fellow marketer who's drowning in work and desperately searching for a better way?

My mission with this book is simple: to show every overwhelmed marketer, stressed business owner, and burnt-out freelancer that there is a path from chaos to clarity using AI tools.

But here's the thing: I need your help to reach them.

Most people pick books based on reviews. They're looking for someone like them who says, "This actually works." That someone could be you.

Your review takes two minutes but could save someone from:

- Another 80-hour work week
- Missing their kid's game because of a "quick" campaign revision
- Losing a client because they can't keep up
- Giving up on their business dreams

Instead, your review could help them:

- Finally leave the office before dinner
- Scale their business without burning out
- Compete with companies 10x their size
- Actually enjoy marketing again

Remember my son Scott? He was told that he either had a staffing problem or an efficiency problem. And since they weren't going to add more staff, he had an efficiency problem. I'm helping him implement the AI strategies in this book. Your review could help another "Scott" find that same freedom.

Ready to pay it forward? Here's how:

Simply scan this QR code:

What to share in your review:

- Which chapter helped you most
- One specific result you achieved
- Who you'd recommend this book to
- Your honest experience (good or challenging)

You know that satisfaction of helping a colleague solve a problem they've been struggling with? That's what your review does, except you help hundreds of marketers at once.

From one marketer to another, thank you for taking two minutes to light the path for someone else.

Here's to fewer late nights and more breakthrough moments,

Brian Duvall

P.S. If this book saved you even one hour this week, your review could save someone else an entire career of frustration. That's the power of sharing what works.

CHAPTER 7
THE COUNTDOWN BEGINS: LAUNCHING WITH AI PRECISION

"THE WEBSITE'S DOWN! The payment system's not working! Where's the email that was supposed to go out? Why is the Facebook ad still showing the old price?"

Launch day, 2021, at 4:17 PM. Everything that could go wrong was going wrong.

That story plays out across all industries. Your client's course launch turned into a masterclass in chaos. Many marketers recover (barely), but the stress takes years off your life.

Today? You can launch five products in one week. Zero crashes. Zero panic. Smooth as Tennessee whiskey.

The difference? AI-powered launch systems that anticipate problems before they happen.

THE LAUNCH PARADOX NOBODY TALKS ABOUT

Here's the dirty secret of marketing launches: The more successful your pre-launch, the more likely your launch is to fail.

Why? Because success brings complexity:

- More traffic than your systems can handle
- More questions than your team can answer
- More edge cases than you anticipated
- More opportunities for Murphy's Law

AI doesn't eliminate these challenges. It helps you see them coming and prepare accordingly.

THE THREE-PHASE LAUNCH SYSTEM THAT ACTUALLY WORKS

Forget the traditional "build hype and hope" approach. Modern launches need:

1. **Intelligent Preparation** (Weeks -4 to -1)
2. **Adaptive Execution** (Launch week)
3. **Rapid Optimization** (Post-launch)

Let me show you how each phase works with AI...

PHASE 1: INTELLIGENT PREPARATION

The best launches are won before they begin. Here's how AI transforms preparation:

The Content Multiplication Machine

Remember creating unique content for every day of launch? I once spent a week writing launch emails. By launch day, I was so burnt out I could barely function.

Now? I can spend 4 hours creating templates and have AI handle the rest.

The Launch Content Generator Prompt:

"You are a highly effective product launch expert. Help me launch [product] on [date]. Target audience: [description] Key benefit: [what they get] Big promise: [transformation offered] Price point: [details] Urgency factor: [why buy now]

Create a 10-day launch sequence:

- Days -7 to -4: Build awareness of the problem
- Days -3 to -2: Tease the solution
- Day -1: Major reveal
- Day 0: Launch announcement
- Days 1-3: Handle objections and add bonuses

For each day, write:

1. Email subject and preview text
2. Social media post (casual tone)
3. SMS message (urgent but not pushy)

Maintain excitement while addressing different buyer personalities."

The Tech Stack Stress Test

AI can't fix your servers, but it can predict when they'll break.

Pre-Launch Technical Audit:

- Load testing with AI traffic simulation
- Payment flow testing with edge cases
- Email deliverability checks
- Mobile experience optimization

Companies use AI to generate hundreds of test scenarios: What if someone has a hyphen in their name? Uses an emoji in the form? Tries to buy from Antarctica? Catches issues humans miss.

The Question Prediction Engine

Every launch generates the same 20 questions 100 times. AI helps you prepare.

Feed past customer support tickets into ChatGPT: "Analyze these support conversations from previous launches. Identify:

1. Top 10 questions customers will ask
2. Emotional state when asking
3. Best responses that led to purchases
4. Create an FAQ that preempts these issues."

Try it on your next launch and watch your support tickets drop by as much as 73%.

PHASE 2: ADAPTIVE EXECUTION

Launch day isn't a sprint; it's a chess match. AI helps you think five moves ahead.

The Real-Time Response System

While you're handling the big picture, AI manages the details:

Auto-Responders That Feel Human:

- Different responses based on question sentiment
- Escalation to humans for complex issues
- Follow-up sequences for non-purchasers
- Thank you sequences for buyers

The Response Framework:

If a question contains [pricing, cost, expensive]:

→ Respond with value emphasis + payment plan option

If a question contains [technical, setup, difficult]:

→ Respond with simplicity assurance + setup support offer

If a question contains [guarantee, refund, risk]:

→ Respond with guarantee details + success stories

The Traffic Controller

If your website crashes due to traffic spikes, then use web hosting with AI traffic shaping:

1. **Monitor in Real-Time**: AI watches server loads
2. **Predict Surge Patterns**: Based on email open rates and social engagement
3. **Adapt Automatically**: Throttle non-essential features during peaks
4. **Queue Management**: "You're 47th in line" beats a crashed site

One company had 50,000 simultaneous visitors. Their site never slowed down.

The Conversion Optimization Loop

Traditional approach: Launch, pray, analyze later. AI approach: Optimize while the iron's hot.

Live Launch Optimization:

- A/B test headlines hourly
- Adjust urgency messaging based on conversion rates
- Personalize offers based on behavior
- Shift budget to winning channels instantly

PHASE 3: RAPID POST-LAUNCH OPTIMIZATION

The sale ends. Most marketers collapse, but savvy marketers double down.

The Buyer Intelligence Goldmine

Every purchaser tells you how to find the next one. AI helps you listen:

"Analyze these customer profiles who purchased during launch:

1. What do they have in common?
2. What channels drove the highest-value customers?

3. What messaging resonated most?
4. Where can we find more like them?"

This intelligence feeds your next campaign.

The Non-Buyer Rescue System

More valuable than buyers? People who almost bought.

AI segments non-buyers:

- **Price Sensitive**: Gets payment plan offer
- **Need More Proof**: Gets case study sequence
- **Technical Concerns**: Gets demo and support offer
- **Bad Timing**: Gets "next cohort" early bird list

We typically convert 15-20% of non-buyers within 30 days.

The Mars & Amazon Story That Changes Everything

Mars (yes, the candy company) partnered with Amazon for a campaign that shows AI's launch power at scale.

The Challenge: Celebrate everyday consumer achievements with personalized experiences.

The AI Solution:

- Processed 60,000+ submissions automatically
- Created personalized responses for each
- Integrated with Amazon's ordering system
- Managed logistics at a massive scale

The Results:

- 4.3% sales increase post-campaign
- 92% brand awareness (2-point jump)
- 72% ad recall with Gen Z

The lesson? AI enables personalization at scale that would be impossible manually. [1]

Launch Leaders: The Innovation Playbook

BMW: Used AI to create localized launch content across multiple countries. It's the same campaign, perfectly adapted for each market. [2]

Nutella: 7 million unique AI-generated labels. Sold out in a month. Proof that personalization drives urgency. [3]

Heinz: AI-generated ketchup art campaign. 1.15 billion impressions. 38% higher engagement than traditional campaigns. [4]

Coca-Cola: Combined AI creative tools for user-generated holiday campaigns. 120,000 pieces of content created by consumers. [5]

Pattern recognition: Leaders use AI to make launches interactive, not just transactional.

YOUR LAUNCH COMMAND CENTER SETUP

Here's the exact tech stack for stress-free launches:

For Project Management:

- **Trello + Butler**: Automates task creation and reminders
- **Notion**: Central knowledge base with AI assist
- **Slack**: With AI bots for instant answers

For Content Creation:

- **ChatGPT/Claude**: Copy generation and variation
- **Canva**: Visual content with Magic Design
- **Loom**: Quick explainer videos with AI transcripts

For Technical Infrastructure:

- **Carrd + Stripe**: Simple, reliable checkout
- **Make.com**: Connects everything automatically

- **Google Tag Manager**: Track everything without code

For Customer Communication:

- **Intercom or Drift**: AI chatbots with human escalation
- **MailerLite**: Email automation with AI optimization
- **Twilio**: SMS with intelligent routing

Total setup time: One weekend. Peace of mind: Priceless.

ADVANCED LAUNCH STRATEGIES

Strategy 1: The Rolling Thunder Launch

Instead of one big day, create multiple peaks:

- Monday: VIP early access
- Wednesday: Public launch
- Friday: Bonus addition
- Sunday: Final call

AI adjusts messaging and urgency for each phase.

Strategy 2: The Scarcity Reality Show

Document your inventory/spots in real time:

- "47 left..."
- "Jessica from Portland just claimed hers..."
- "Only 12 remaining..."

AI updates across all channels simultaneously. Real scarcity, ethically communicated.

Strategy 3: The Choose Your Adventure Launch

Let customers pick their path:

- "I want to learn more" → Education sequence
- "I'm ready but have questions" → FAQ and chat
- "Show me the deal" → Direct to offer

AI personalizes everything after based on their choice.

COMMON LAUNCH MISTAKES (LEARN FROM MY PAIN)

Mistake 1: Testing in Production

"We'll fix it live" = "We'll lose customers live"

Fix: AI-powered staging environments that simulate real conditions.

Mistake 2: The Kitchen Sink Launch

Trying to appeal to everyone waters down your message.

Fix: AI helps segment and personalize without diluting the core offer.

Mistake 3: Abandoning Ship Post-Launch

The first 48 hours after launch are gold for optimization.

Fix: AI monitoring and adjustment tools that work while you sleep.

THE PSYCHOLOGY OF SUCCESSFUL LAUNCHES

Launches aren't about features or benefits. They're about moments:

- The moment someone realizes they need to change
- The moment they believe change is possible
- The moment they decide you're the one to help
- The moment they overcome their final objection

AI helps orchestrate these moments at scale.

Your Pre-Launch Checklist

Two weeks before launch:

- [ ] Tech stack tested under load
- [ ] Support responses prepared for the top 20 questions
- [ ] Content created for 10-day sequence
- [ ] Tracking systems verified
- [ ] Team briefed on escalation procedures

One week before:

- [ ] Early bird list warmed up
- [ ] Partners/affiliates prepared
- [ ] Social media scheduled
- [ ] Backup systems ready
- [ ] Celebration planned (seriously)

Launch day:

- [ ] Coffee ready
- [ ] AI systems monitoring
- [ ] Team on standby
- [ ] Expectations realistic
- [ ] Ready to adapt

THE ONE QUESTION THAT MATTERS

Before any launch, ask: "What would have to be true for this to feel easy?"

Then, use AI to make those things true.

For my wedding venue client, "easy" meant automated FAQ responses. For the cosmetic dentist, "easy" meant appointment booking that just worked. For the software company, "easy" meant qualified leads only.

Define your "easy." AI will help you achieve it.

Your Launch Challenge

Before reading the next chapter:

1. List your last launch's biggest stress point
2. Find one AI tool that could eliminate it
3. Calculate the ROI of stress reduction (hint: it's huge)

Remember: Smooth launches aren't about perfection. They're about preparation and adaptation. AI gives you both.

Coming up: The launch was a success! Now what? Chapter 8 reveals how AI transforms post-launch data into your next breakthrough.

CHAPTER 8
THE OPTIMIZATION SYMPHONY: ORCHESTRATING SUCCESS WITH AI ANALYTICS

"BRIAN, I have good news and bad news."

My client's voice crackled through the phone. It was week three after their product launch.

"Good news: We hit our sales target. Bad news: I have no idea why. Our analytics show traffic from everywhere, conversions at random times, and I can't tell which marketing actually worked."

Sound familiar? You pour money into marketing, and sales happen, but connecting cause to effect feels like solving a mystery with half the clues missing.

That was early in my career. Today? Clients know exactly which social media story drove $12,000 in sales last Tuesday at 3:47 PM.

The difference isn't more data. It's AI making sense of the data you already have.

THE ANALYTICS PARADOX THAT'S KILLING YOUR ROI

Here's the modern marketing contradiction: We have more data than ever, yet we feel less confident in our decisions.

Why? Because human brains weren't designed to process:

- 47 different metrics across 12 platforms
- Customer journeys with 38 touchpoints
- Attribution models that would make statisticians cry
- Real-time optimization decisions every hour

We're drowning in numbers while thirsting for insights.

THE THREE LEVELS OF MARKETING INTELLIGENCE

After analyzing hundreds of campaigns, I've found businesses operate at one of three levels:

Level 1: Vanity Metrics "We got 10,000 impressions!" (So what?) "Our followers grew 25%!" (Did revenue?) "Open rates are up!" (Are sales?)

Level 2: Activity Metrics "Cost per click is $2.50" (Is that good?) "Conversion rate is 3%" (For which audience?) "Email drives most traffic" (But does it drive profit?)

Level 3: Intelligence Metrics "Customers who read case studies convert 47% better" "Tuesday emails to segment B drive 3x revenue" "Instagram stories between 2-4 PM produce highest ROI"

AI takes you from Level 1 to Level 3 without a PhD in data science.

BUILDING YOUR AI ANALYTICS COMMAND CENTER

Forget dashboards that just display data. You need systems that generate decisions.

The Data Integration Challenge

The Old Way:

- Log into Google Analytics (5 minutes)
- Export Facebook Ads data (5 minutes)
- Check email platform (5 minutes)
- Copy into a spreadsheet (10 minutes)
- Try to make sense of it (2 hours)
- Give up and guess (30 seconds)

The AI Way: One dashboard. All insights. Actual recommendations. Experiment with this exact setup:

1. **Looker Studio** as the central hub
2. **Supermetrics** pulling data from all platforms
3. **ChatGPT/Claude** analyzing trends and anomalies
4. **Automated alerts** for significant changes

Time investment: 2 hours to set up, 15 minutes weekly to review.

THE INSIGHT GENERATION PROMPT THAT CHANGES EVERYTHING

Every Monday, feed your metrics into AI with this prompt:

"You are a marketing data analyst. Analyze this marketing performance data from last week: [Paste key metrics]

Compare to the previous 4-week average: [Paste historical data]

Business context:

- We launched [X] on [date]
- Our goal is [specific target]
- Budget constraints: [details]

Identify:

1. The single biggest insight hiding in this data
2. What's working better than expected (and why)
3. What's underperforming (and likely cause)
4. Three specific actions to take this week
5. What metrics should we watch the closest

Be specific with numbers and reasoning."

This prompt can identify opportunities worth millions. Literally.

DELTA'S $30 MILLION DISCOVERY

Let me share a story that shows what's possible when AI meets marketing analytics.

Delta Air Lines had a problem every big brand faces: They spent millions on brand advertising (Olympics sponsorship, anyone?) but couldn't connect it to ticket sales.

Traditional attribution said: "Brand advertising drives awareness." CFO translation: "You're wasting money on things we can't measure."

Enter AI-powered analytics.

The Transformation:

- Fed TV ad data, social mentions, search trends, and sales into AI
- Spiking Neural Networks found hidden correlations
- Connected Paris Olympics sponsorship to specific route bookings
- Identified which creative elements drove purchase intent

The $30 Million Result: They proved their Olympics sponsorship directly drove $30 million in ticket sales. Not "maybe influenced." Directly drove.

The lesson? Your marketing impact is bigger than your spreadsheets show. AI helps prove it. [1]

The Optimization Playbook Industry Leaders Use

BMW + IBM Watson: 30% increase in social engagement by analyzing sentiment and adjusting content in real-time. Your version? Use ChatGPT to analyze your post comments weekly. [2]

Coca-Cola: AI reduces marketing costs while improving engagement by predicting which content will resonate. Your play? Test 10 variations and let AI identify patterns in winners. [3]

ADVANCED OPTIMIZATION STRATEGIES

Strategy 1: The Micro-Cohort Method

Instead of optimizing for "all customers," AI helps identify micro-cohorts:

- "Lawyers in Texas who visit pricing twice"
- "E-commerce owners who read customer stories"
- "Morning email openers who click social proof"

When optimized for 12 micro-cohorts, the overall conversion rate went from 2.1% to 5.7%.

Strategy 2: The Sentiment-Success Correlation:

AI analyzes the emotional tone of your content in relation to conversion rates.

Discovery: Our shutter manufacturing client's "aggressive" sales emails had 50% lower lifetime value customers than "educational" ones. Those two campaigns had the same initial conversion rate but vastly different long-term values.

Strategy 3: The Competitive Intelligence Loop

AI monitors competitor changes and correlates with your performance:

- Competitor raises prices → Your conversion rate improves
- Competitor launches feature → Specific segment shows concern
- Competitor changes messaging → Your positioning opportunity

It's like having a spy in their marketing meetings (legally).

The Metrics That Actually Predict Success

Stop tracking everything. Start tracking what matters:

The North Star Metrics

For SaaS: Trial → Paid Conversion Rate (by source)

For E-commerce: Repeat Purchase Rate (by category)

For Services: Qualified Conversation Rate (by channel)

For Local: Appointment Show Rate (by campaign)

Everything else is a supporting cast.

The Leading Indicators

These predict future success:

- **Engagement Velocity**: How fast someone moves through your funnel
- **Multi-Touch Rate**: How many times they interact before buying
- **Share Rate**: How often they tell others (organic amplification)
- **Question Quality**: Support questions shifting from "what" to "how"

AI excels at spotting these patterns before humans notice.

Your Optimization Audit Framework

Every month, run this audit:

The Performance Forensics

1. **What moved the needle?**
    - Which specific actions drove results?
    - Can we do more of it?
    - What was the true cost?
2. **What was noise?**
    - Which activities generated activity but not outcomes?
    - Can we do less of it?
    - What could we test instead?
3. **What surprised us?**
    - Which assumptions were wrong?
    - What patterns did AI find that we missed?
    - How do we adjust strategy?

The Optimization Hit List

Based on the audit, create your hit list:

1. **Quick Wins**: Changes you can make today
2. **Test Queue**: Hypotheses worth validating
3. **Strategic Shifts**: Bigger changes requiring planning

AI helps prioritize by predicted impact.

COMMON ANALYTICS MISTAKES (AND AI FIXES)

Mistake 1: Optimizing for the Wrong Metric

Chasing low customer acquisition costs (CAC) might get you bad customers.

AI Fix: Multi-metric optimization that balances cost, quality, and lifetime value.

Mistake 2: Analysis Paralysis

So much data, so little action.

AI Fix: Force-rank recommendations by predicted ROI.

Mistake 3: Correlation vs. Causation Confusion

Ice cream sales and drownings both increase in summer, but one does not cause the other.

AI Fix: Use AI to run virtual experiments and validate causation.

The Real-Time Optimization Revolution

Here's what's possible today that wasn't possible just a few years ago.

Dynamic Budget Allocation: AI shifts spending each hour based on performance

Creative Fatigue Detection: Knows when ads are wearing out before your click-through rate (CTR) drops

Predictive Trend Alerts: "Your costs will spike next week because..."

Automated Response: Changes bids, budgets, and creative without needing your time and attention

We had a client's AI system prevent a $50K loss by pausing campaigns before a platform glitch. The AI saw anomalies humans missed.

BUILDING YOUR AI ANALYTICS PRACTICE

Week 1: Foundation

- Connect all data sources to the central dashboard
- Set up basic automated reporting
- Establish baseline metrics

Week 2: Intelligence Layer

- Add AI analysis to weekly reviews
- Create alert systems for anomalies

- Test first optimization recommendations

Week 3: Automation

- Implement auto-adjusting budgets
- Create dynamic creative testing
- Build feedback loops

Week 4: Advanced Analytics

- Develop predictive models
- Test micro-cohort optimization
- Plan strategic experiments

The Psychology of Data-Driven Decisions

Here's the hard truth: Most of us make emotional decisions and then find data to support them.

AI doesn't care about your pet campaigns. It doesn't have an ego to protect. It just finds what works.

That objectivity is its superpower, and that's why it's sometimes hard to accept its recommendations.

Your Analytics Transformation Checklist

Before moving on:

- [ ] Can you explain your funnel metrics in one sentence?
- [ ] Do you know your actual customer acquisition cost by channel?
- [ ] Can you predict next month's performance within 10%?
- [ ] Are you optimizing for leading or lagging indicators?
- [ ] When did you last kill an underperforming campaign?

If you answered "no" to any of these, AI can help fix it this week.

The One Analytics Question That Matters

"If I could only know three things about my marketing performance, what would indicate if we're winning or losing?"

For the wedding venue: Booking rate, average order value, lead source. For the software company: Trial starts, activation rate, expansion revenue. For the dental practice: New patient calls, show rate, treatment acceptance

Define your three. Optimize relentlessly. Ignore the noise.

Your Optimization Challenge

This week:

1. Run the performance forensics audit
2. Feed results into AI for analysis
3. Implement one recommended change
4. Measure the impact

Start small. Even a 5% improvement compounds into breakthrough results.

Coming up: You've optimized what's working. Now it's time to scale. Chapter 9 reveals how AI transforms small wins into massive victories.

CHAPTER 9
THE SCALING STRATOSPHERE: ACCELERATING GROWTH WITH AI INTELLIGENCE

YOU'RE PROFITABLE, growing 30% monthly, but you're working 80-hour weeks just to keep up. So, how do you scale without everything falling apart?

That question haunts every successful business: How do you grow without breaking what got you there?

THE SCALING PARADOX NOBODY WARNS YOU ABOUT

Here's what they don't teach in business school: The strategies that get you from 0 to 1 rarely work from 1 to 10. And what works from 1 to 10 almost never works from 10 to 100.

I learned this brutally with Smart Business Development. Our scrappy guerrilla marketing efforts, which initially built traction, completely failed when we tried to scale. What worked for finding 100 customers couldn't find 10,000.

Why? Because scaling isn't about doing more of the same. It's about the fundamental transformation of how you operate.

THE THREE TYPES OF SCALE

Linear Scaling: More input = proportionally more output

- Hire more people, get more done
- Spend more on ads, get more clicks
- Problem: these eventually hit a wall

Leveraged Scaling: Better systems = multiplied output

- Better processes, higher efficiency
- Better targeting, higher conversion
- Problem: Still has human limitations

Exponential Scaling: AI-enabled systems = compound growth

- Self-improving algorithms
- Network effects
- Autonomous optimization
- Problem: Requires fundamental rethinking

Most businesses stuck in linear thinking wonder why growth gets harder. AI enables the jump to exponential.

THE STACKBLITZ TRANSFORMATION THAT CHANGED EVERYTHING

Let me share a story that illustrates exponential scaling in action.

StackBlitz was dying. End of 2023, they had:

- Lackluster revenue
- Minimal growth
- Limited resources
- Headed for failure

Then, they made one strategic decision: Put AI at the core of their product (Bolt.new), not just their marketing.

The Results:

- 30 days: $4 million Annually Renewable Revenue (ARR)
- 5 months: $40 million ARR
- 10x growth in 150 days
- With the same small team

That's not improvement. That's transformation.

WHAT STACKBLITZ DID DIFFERENTLY

Traditional Scaling: "How do we get more developers to use our tools?"

Their Approach: "How do we help non-developers build like developers?"

By embedding AI (Claude Sonnet 3.5) into their product, they didn't just improve their market position; they created an entirely new market. [1]

Key lessons:

1. They solved a bigger problem (democratizing development)
2. They leveraged AI for customer value, not just efficiency
3. They created network effects (users sharing AI-built apps)
4. They made their product indispensable, not just useful

THE SCALING INTELLIGENCE FRAMEWORK

After studying dozens of AI-powered scaling stories, here's the framework that works:

Phase 1: Foundation Analysis (Weeks 1-2)

Before scaling anything, understand what's actually working.

The Funnel Forensics Deep Dive:

Use this prompt with your analytics:

"Analyze this complete funnel data:

- Traffic sources: [data]
- Conversion points: [data]
- Customer journey: [data]
- Revenue by segment: [data]

Identify:

1. The 20% of efforts driving 80% of results
2. Hidden bottlenecks limiting growth
3. Untapped opportunities in current traffic
4. Which segments have the highest growth potential
5. What would break first if we 10x volume

Provide specific recommendations ranked by impact."

Phase 2: Intelligence Amplification (Weeks 3-4)

Don't just do more. Do smarter.

The Three Amplifiers:

1. **Precision Targeting**: AI identifies your best customers' twins
2. **Message Optimization**: AI personalizes at scale
3. **Channel Efficiency**: AI allocates resources dynamically

Real example: An E-learning company used AI to identify that customers who watched their free webinar past minute 37 were 8 times more likely to buy. They restructured their offer reveal for minute 38. Sales tripled.

Phase 3: Systematic Scaling (Weeks 5-8)

Now, scale what works and cut what doesn't.

The S.C.A.L.E. Method

Segment: Divide your market into specific cohorts

Customize: Tailor your approach for each segment

Automate: Remove the human bottlenecks

Learn: Feed the results back into the system

Expand: Apply what you learned to new segments

Industry Leaders Show Exponential Growth

Cursor (Anysphere): $100 million ARR in 21 months with 20 people. How? AI-native coding assistant that makes every developer 10 times more productive. [2]

MidJourney: $200 million+ ARR in 2 years with a lean team. Secret? They made professional image creation accessible to everyone. [3]

ElevenLabs: $90 million+ ARR with ~50 people. Method? AI voice technology that's so good it enables entirely new use cases. [4]

Pattern? They don't just use AI to improve existing processes. They use it to enable what was previously impossible.

ADVANCED SCALING STRATEGIES

Strategy 1: The Product-Led Growth Accelerator

Instead of scaling marketing, scale the product's ability to market itself.

Example: Notion, a popular note-taking app, added AI summarization. Users started sharing AI summaries publicly. Each share brought 3-5 new users. Their viral coefficient went from 0.3 to 1.4. [5]

Strategy 2: The Competitive Moat Builder

Use AI to create advantages competitors can't easily copy.

HireVue, a recruiting firm, built AI that learned from every successful placement. After 1,000 placements, their matching accuracy was three times better than that of their competitors. That advantage compounds daily. [6]

Strategy 3: The Market Creation Play

Don't compete for existing demand. Create new categories.

StackBlitz didn't compete with developer tools. They created "AI-powered instant development environments." New category = no direct competition.

THE SCALING METRICS THAT MATTER

Forget vanity metrics. Track scaling health:

Efficiency Metrics:

- Revenue per Employee
- Customer Acquisition Cost Trend
- Lifetime Value to CAC Ratio
- Time to Revenue for New Initiatives

Scalability Metrics:

- Viral Coefficient
- Net Revenue Retention
- Automation Percentage
- AI-Driven Revenue Percentage

Health Metrics:

- Employee Burnout Score
- System Stress Points
- Customer Satisfaction at Scale
- Technical Debt Accumulation

YOUR SCALING READINESS AUDIT

Before attempting scale, answer honestly:

Product-Market Fit:

- [ ] Customers actively recommend you
- [ ] Churn is predictable and manageable
- [ ] You're turning away business
- [ ] Expansion revenue exists

Operational Readiness:

- [ ] Core processes are documented
- [ ] Key metrics are automated
- [ ] Team can handle 2x volume
- [ ] Systems can handle 10x volume

Strategic Clarity:

- [ ] Clear ideal customer profile
- [ ] Proven unit economics
- [ ] Identified scaling channels
- [ ] AI enhancement opportunities mapped

Score less than 10/12? Fix foundations before scaling.

COMMON SCALING MISTAKES (AND AI SOLUTIONS)

Mistake 1: Scaling Before Product-Market Fit

Like putting rocket engines on a bicycle.

AI Fix: Use AI to analyze customer feedback and identify your true Product Market Fit (PMF) signals.

Mistake 2: Linear Thinking in Exponential Times

Hiring 10 times more people to get 10 times the results.

AI Fix: Find the 10x leverage points in your business model.

Mistake 3: Ignoring Compound Effects

Not recognizing which improvements compound vs. one-time gains.

AI Fix: Model the long-term impact of various scaling strategies.

THE SCALING TRANSFORMATION PLAYBOOK

Month 1: Intelligence Gathering

- Complete funnel analysis
- Identify scaling bottlenecks
- Map AI enhancement opportunities
- Set exponential goals

Month 2: Foundation Building

- Implement core AI systems
- Automate repetitive processes
- Establish feedback loops
- Test scaling hypotheses

Month 3: Acceleration

- Double down on what works
- Cut what doesn't scale
- Add fuel to winners
- Monitor system stress

Months 4-6: Exponential Growth

- Compound improvements daily
- Expand to new segments

- Build competitive moats
- Plan next evolution

The Psychology of Exponential Thinking

Here's what held me back for years: I was thinking arithmetically in a geometric world.

Adding more hours, more people, and more budget, that's arithmetic thinking. Building systems that improve themselves, that's geometric thinking.

AI forces geometric thinking because it:

- Learns from every interaction
- Improves without human intervention
- Scales without proportional costs
- Compounds knowledge over time

Your Scaling Challenge

This week, identify:

1. Your single biggest scaling bottleneck
2. How AI could 10x (not 10%) improve it
3. The smallest test to validate the approach

Remember: Scaling isn't about working harder. It's about building systems that work harder for you.

The One Scaling Question That Matters

"What would need to be true for our business to grow 10x with the same size team?"

For StackBlitz, it was making development accessible to non-developers. For MidJourney, it was making design accessible to non-designers. For your business, it might be making [your expertise] accessible to [new audiences].

That's where exponential growth lives, in expanding the definition of who can benefit from what you offer.

Coming up: You've scaled to new heights. Now, how do you keep customers for life? Chapter 10 reveals how AI transforms one-time buyers into lifetime advocates.

CHAPTER 10
THE LOYALTY LABORATORY: ENGINEERING RETENTION WITH AI INTELLIGENCE

"WE'RE GROWING FAST, but I feel like we're filling a bucket with holes in it."

The SaaS founder's confession hit close to home. They were acquiring 1,000 new customers monthly but losing 400. Do the math, that's 40% churn. At that rate, they'd need to acquire 12,000 customers just to net 7,200 by year-end.

I see this pattern everywhere: Businesses obsess over acquisition while retention bleeds them dry.

Here's the brutal truth I learned managing cold calling operations at SalesHive: It costs 5-25 times more to acquire a new customer than to keep an existing one. Yet most marketing budgets are 90% acquisition and 10% retention.

That's like pouring water into a bucket while ignoring the giant hole in the bottom.

THE RETENTION REVOLUTION NOBODY'S TALKING ABOUT

Traditional retention was reactive:

- Wait for customers to complain
- Send generic "We miss you" emails
- Offer desperate discounts to win them back
- Hope for the best

AI-powered retention is predictive:

- Know who's at risk before they do
- Personalize interventions based on behavior
- Address specific concerns proactively
- Turn potential churners into advocates

The difference? One fights fires. The other prevents them.

THE THREE PILLARS OF AI-POWERED RETENTION

Pillar 1: Intelligent Onboarding Get them to value fast

Pillar 2: Predictive Risk Detection Spot trouble before it happens

Pillar 3: Proactive Success Systems Make their success inevitable

Let me show you how each works.

Pillar 1: The First 14 Days That Determine Everything

Your relationship with a customer is won or lost in the first two weeks. Yet, most onboarding feels like being handed an IKEA manual in Swedish.

The Onboarding Transformation

Traditional Onboarding: Day 1: "Welcome! Here's everything about our product!" (Overwhelming) Day 3: "Did you see our welcome email?" (Naggy) Day 7: "Check out these 47 features!" (Desperate) Day 14: Customer ghosts you (Predictable)

AI-Powered Onboarding:

The following was built for a project management software company:

Day 1: AI analyzes signup data (company size, industry, role)

- Enterprise CEO gets: "Quick win: Set up your first executive dashboard (3 min)"
- Startup founder gets: "Quick win: Create your first project template (3 min)"

Day 3: AI checks usage patterns

- Power-user gets advanced tips
- Struggler gets a personal video walkthrough
- Non-user gets "Stuck? Here's the one thing to try."

Day 7: AI identifies their "Aha!" moment

- Triggered when they experience core value
- Reinforces what they did right
- Shows logical next step

Day 14: AI predicts success likelihood

- High probability: Upsell to an annual plan
- Medium probability: Offer coaching session
- Result? The activation rate went from 34% to 71%.

The Behavioral Trigger Map

Try this AI prompt to revolutionize your onboarding:

"Role: You are a customer onboarding expert. Analyze these customer success patterns:

- Successful customers who stayed 12+ months: [behaviors]
- Customers who churned in first 90 days: [behaviors]

Identify:

1. The earliest behavioral indicators of success
2. The 'point of no return' for churn risk
3. Specific interventions that correlate with retention
4. Optimal timing for each intervention
5. Personalization variables that matter most

Create an onboarding journey that maximizes success indicators."

Pillar 2: The Crystal Ball of Customer Health

Waiting for customers to cancel is like waiting for chest pains to prevent a heart attack. AI gives you the EKG.

Hydrant's AI-Powered Churn Prediction Engine

Hydrant, a consumer wellness product company, implemented an AI-powered churn prediction system that identifies early warning signals and prescribes targeted remediation strategies, very similar to your meal delivery example.

The Challenge: Hydrant's email marketing wasn't properly segmented, and they needed to identify customers at risk of churning before it was too late.

AI Early Warning System: Hydrant used Pecan AI's predictive modeling to study churn in their customer base. Their churn report, built in just two weeks, helped identify three key customer segments:

- Customers with a high probability of making a repeat purchase
- Customers likely to transition from one-time purchases to subscription models
- Former customers who could be persuaded to make another purchase

Prescriptive Actions: Like your example, the AI didn't just flag risks—it prescribed targeted campaigns for different customer segments based on their churn likelihood and behavior patterns.

Results:

- **260% higher conversion rate** for targeted retention campaigns
- **310% increase in revenue per customer** through AI-driven interventions
- Over 83% of customers identified as likely to churn did actually churn, proving the model's accuracy

Key Insight: Hydrant didn't waste resources on customers who were "halfway out the door" and instead focused their efforts on customers who could be retained through targeted interventions. [1]

The Risk Segmentation Matrix

Not all churn risks are equal. AI helps prioritize:

Red Alert (Immediate action):

- High LTV customers showing multiple risk signals
- Influencers or reference customers at risk
- Customers near renewal showing disengagement

Yellow Warning (Proactive nurture):

- Medium-value customers with a single-risk signal
- New customers not reaching activation milestones
- Seasonal users entering the off-season

Green Monitor (Automated care):

- Low-risk customers with minor issues
- Natural usage fluctuations within the normal range
- Self-service users preferring minimal contact

Pillar 3: Success Systems That Scale

What is the best retention strategy? Make customers so successful they can't imagine leaving.

The Proactive Success Playbook

Hydrant's approach inspired this framework:

Layer 1: Intelligent Support

- AI chatbots handle 80% of routine questions
- Complex issues escalate with full context
- Proactive tips based on usage patterns

Layer 2: Predictive Personalization

- AI learns individual preferences
- Suggests products before they ask
- Celebrates milestones and progress

Layer 3: Community Connection

- Matches customers with similar goals
- Facilitates peer support and advice
- Creates belonging beyond the product

Real example: Intercom's AI-Powered Customer Success Framework

Intercom, a leading customer service platform with over 25,000 customers, has implemented a comprehensive three-layer framework using Claude AI that closely mirrors your "Proactive Success Playbook."

Layer 1: Intelligent Support (Fin AI Agent)

- Resolves up to 86% of customer support volume with human-quality responses
- Achieves 51% average resolution rate out of the box
- Reduces response times from 30 minutes to seconds
- Handles routine inquiries in 45+ languages, allowing human agents to focus on complex issues

Layer 2: Predictive Personalization

- Fin learns everything about each company's products and services using their entire knowledge base
- Adapts communication style to match each business's tone and policies
- Provides personalized answer length and policy-aware responses
- Takes proactive actions like processing refunds and managing account changes

Layer 3: Strategic Insights and Enhanced Human Collaboration

- AI-generated analytics provide visibility across entire support operations
- Enables support teams to "move up the value chain" and focus on strategic work
- Creates a feedback loop where insights improve the overall system performance
- Elevates human agents from routine tasks to strategic customer experience work

Documented Results:

- Synthesia: AI resolved over 6,000 conversations, saved 1,300+ hours, achieved 87% self-serve rates
- Fundrise: Automated 50% of support volume with 95% accuracy, reduced seasonal spikes by 50%
- Lightspeed: Achieved 65% resolution rates while agents closed 31% more conversations daily

The Framework's Success: Intercom's approach demonstrates the power of layered AI implementation, starting with intelligent automation, adding predictive personalization, and culminating in strategic insights that enhance human capabilities rather than replace them. [2]

ADVANCED RETENTION STRATEGIES

Strategy 1: The Preemptive Strike

Don't wait for problems. Solve them before they exist.

Example: Salesforce, the renowned SaaS company, found that customers who didn't integrate with their CRM in the first week had a 60% higher churn rate. AI now detects non-integration and triggers:

- Personal integration assistance offer
- Video walkthrough specific to their CRM
- Success story from a similar customer
- Direct line to integration specialist

Integration rate up 40%. Churn down 35%.

Strategy 2: The Surprise and Delight Algorithm

AI identifies optimal moments for unexpected value:

- Just before the typical churn point
- After support frustration
- During success milestones
- Random intervals to break patterns

Netflix's AI-Powered Personalized Retention Strategy

Netflix has implemented a comprehensive AI-driven personalized retention system that closely mirrors the Ipsy example, using individual customer profiles to trigger personalized surprises and experiences that significantly reduce churn.

The AI-Powered Personalization Engine:

- Analyzes thousands of data points per user including viewing habits, time spent watching, device usage, and engagement patterns
- Creates individual risk profiles to identify customers at risk of churning

- Triggers personalized interventions based on individual behavior patterns

AI-Triggered Personalized Interventions:

- **Personalized Content Recommendations**: 80% of watched content comes from AI-generated recommendations tailored to individual preferences
- **Customized Messaging**: Uses phrases like "Based on your interest in..." and "Your taste preferences created this row" to create personal connections
- **Surprise Content Discovery**: Creates unique "altgenres" like "Reluctant Adults" or "Gritty Movies" - Netflix had nearly 77,000 personalized micro-genres in 2014
- **Early Access Perks**: Provides personalized homepage layouts and priority access to content that matches individual viewing patterns

Documented Results:

- **Reduced churn by several percentage points** through personalized retention strategies
- **Saved over $1 billion annually** through AI-powered customer retention
- **90%+ customer retention rate** - significantly higher than competitors like Hulu (64%) and Amazon Prime (75%)
- **Monthly churn rate is very low** with most cancellations due to payment issues, not customer choice
- Users save over **1,300 hours per day** in search time through personalization, leading to increased engagement

The Individual Risk Profile System: Netflix's AI continuously analyzes individual customer behavior to identify early warning signs of potential churn, then automatically triggers personalized retention strategies - exactly like the Ipsy example's approach of using individual risk profiles to determine appropriate interventions.
3

Strategy 3: The Alumni Network

Not all churn is bad. Some customers outgrow you or need change. AI helps maintain relationships:

- Graceful offboarding with future re-engagement hooks
- Alumni perks and community access
- Referral programs for better-fit customers
- Win-back campaigns when circumstances change

B2B client recovers 15% of churned customers within 18 months using AI-powered alumni nurturing.

YOUR RETENTION AUDIT CHECKLIST

Score your current retention system:

Onboarding Excellence:

- [ ] Personalized first experience
- [ ] Clear path to the first value
- [ ] Proactive obstacle removal
- [ ] Success milestone tracking

Risk Detection:

- [ ] Behavioral monitoring beyond usage
- [ ] Predictive modeling for churn
- [ ] Segmented intervention strategies
- [ ] Early warning systems

Success Enablement:

- [ ] Proactive value delivery
- [ ] Intelligent support systems
- [ ] Community building
- [ ] Continuous education

Measurement:

- [ ] Cohort retention tracking
- [ ] Lifetime value optimization
- [ ] Health score accuracy
- [ ] Intervention effectiveness

Score below 12/16? You're leaving money on the table.

COMMON RETENTION MISTAKES (AND AI FIXES)

Mistake 1: One-Size-Fits-All Onboarding

Treating enterprise clients like solopreneurs.

AI Fix: Dynamic onboarding paths based on customer characteristics.

Mistake 2: Reacting to Lagging Indicators

Waiting for the "cancel" button click.

AI Fix: Behavioral prediction models catching risk early.

Mistake 3: Competing on Price

Racing to the bottom with retention discounts.

AI Fix: Value reinforcement based on actual usage data.

The Psychology of Lasting Relationships

Here's what 20 years in business taught me: Customers don't leave products. They leave relationships.

AI doesn't replace human connection. It enables it at scale by:

- Remembering every interaction
- Personalizing every touchpoint
- Anticipating every need
- Celebrating every success

When customers feel seen, known, and valued, price becomes secondary.

YOUR 30-DAY RETENTION TRANSFORMATION

Week 1: Audit Current State

- Map customer journey touchpoints
- Identify churn patterns
- Calculate true retention metrics
- Survey recently churned customers

Week 2: Implement Quick Wins

- Enhance onboarding sequence
- Add behavioral triggers
- Personalize key communications
- Create success milestones

Week 3: Build Predictive Systems

- Set up behavioral tracking
- Create risk scoring model
- Design intervention playbooks
- Test with a small segment

Week 4: Scale and Optimize

- Roll out to the whole customer base
- Monitor leading indicators
- Adjust based on results
- Plan next improvements

The One Retention Question That Matters

"If our customers' success was our only metric, what would we do differently?"

For Hydrant, it meant predicting preferences. For StackBlitz, it meant making development accessible. Imagine what it might mean for your business.

When customer success becomes your north star, retention follows naturally.

Your Retention Challenge

This week:

1. Identify your "golden path," what successful customers do differently
2. Find one moment where customers typically struggle
3. Create an AI-powered intervention for that moment
4. Measure the impact on retention

Start small. Even saving one customer pays for months of AI tools.

Coming up: You've built an incredible retention system. Now, how do you extract insights and preserve knowledge for continuous growth? Chapter 11 reveals how AI transforms feedback into your competitive edge.

CHAPTER 11
THE INSIGHT SYMPHONY: ORCHESTRATING FEEDBACK AND COMMUNICATION WITH AI ANALYTICS

"WE'RE FLYING BLIND." The CMO's frustration was palpable. Despite surveying customers, tracking NPS scores, and monitoring social media, they had no real understanding of what customers actually thought.

"We have data everywhere," she continued, "but no insights anywhere. Our board meetings are just pretty graphs that don't tell us what specifically to do."

I see this constantly. Companies are inundated with feedback but starving for understanding. They collect ratings but miss reasons. Track scores but ignore stories. Measure satisfaction but misunderstand sentiment.

Here's what can change everything for that CMO: AI doesn't just organize feedback. It finds the insights hiding between the lines.

THE FEEDBACK PARADOX MODERN BUSINESSES FACE

We live in the golden age of customer feedback:

- Every interaction rated
- Comments on everything
- Reviews everywhere
- Surveys for days

Yet most businesses know less about customer sentiment than corner stores knew 50 years ago. Why? Because human brains can't process:

- 10,000 support tickets monthly
- 500 survey responses weekly
- 1,000 social mentions daily
- Infinite review variations

We've gone from too little feedback to too much of it to make sense.

THE THREE TYPES OF BUSINESS INTELLIGENCE

Level 1: Data Collection "We track everything!" (But understand nothing)

- Star ratings averaged
- Response rates calculated
- Comments archived
- Dashboards updated

Level 2: Pattern Recognition "We notice trends!" (But miss connections)

- Satisfaction dropping
- Certain features mentioned
- Seasonal variations
- Segment differences

Level 3: Predictive Insights "We see the future!" (And can change it)

- Why satisfaction drops before it does
- Which feedback predicts churn
- Hidden connections between issues
- Opportunities competitors miss

AI takes you from collecting data to predicting outcomes.

BUILDING YOUR FEEDBACK INTELLIGENCE SYSTEM

Forget surveys that nobody reads. Build systems that generate decisions.

The Unified Listening Architecture

Old Way: Feedback silos everywhere

- Support tickets in Zendesk
- Surveys in SurveyMonkey
- Reviews on Google
- Social mentions scattered
- Sales feedback in CRM
- Never shall they meet

AI Way: One intelligence engine

Here's a useful setup that transforms feedback chaos into clarity:

1. **Collection Layer**: All feedback channels feed the central system
2. **Processing Layer**: AI standardizes and categorizes
3. **Analysis Layer**: Pattern recognition across all sources
4. **Insight Layer**: Actionable recommendations generated
5. **Action Layer**: Changes tracked and measured

Investment: One weekend setup. Return: Insights that drove 34% revenue growth.

The Master Analysis Prompt

Every week, feed your unified feedback into AI:

"Analyze this week's customer feedback:

- Support tickets: [data]
- Survey responses: [data]
- Reviews: [data]
- Social mentions: [data]
- Sales team notes: [data]

Context:

- Recent changes: [what we've modified]
- Business priorities: [current focus]
- Known issues: [what we're working on]

Identify:

1. The #1 insight we're missing
2. Emerging issues before they explode
3. Hidden connections between feedback sources
4. Specific customer quotes that illustrate key themes
5. Three actions that would most impact satisfaction

Prioritize by business impact, not volume of mentions."

This prompt catches problems that can cost millions if missed.

The Scandinavian Biolabs Feedback Revolution Let me share how a hair-care brand gets feedback right (and what we can steal).

Scandinavian Biolabs collects thousands of data points:

- Every support ticket
- Every customer complaint
- Every product review
- Every churn signal

But data isn't insight. Here's their genius move:

The AI Transformation:

- Fed all feedback into SentiSum's AI sentiment analysis
- Created 55 custom tags automatically using machine learning
- Found patterns humans were missing in support conversations
- Identified churn drivers before customers actually left

Results:

- 50% reduction in biggest customer dissatisfaction driver
- 50% faster resolution times (from 2 hours to 1 hour) • 19% decrease in generic price enquiries through better documentation
- Product roadmap reprioritized based on actual customer pain points. [1]

Your Version: You don't need Biolab's budget. Free tools + effective prompts = similar insights.

Example: Costa Coffee deployed AI-enhanced QR codes across all tables to analyze customer data. Discovered that personalized promotional campaigns during off-peak hours drive 3x more engagement than generic offers. So, they created targeted AI-driven campaigns based on customer preferences and behavior patterns. Sales during off-peak hours increased by 20%. [2]

ADVANCED FEEDBACK STRATEGIES

Strategy 1: The Sentiment Trajectory Mapping

Don't just measure sentiment; track its direction.

The following was built for a B2B software company:

- AI analyzes each customer's feedback over time
- Maps sentiment trajectory (improving/declining/stable)
- Predicts future state based on patterns

- Triggers interventions for declining trajectories

It caught 73% of churns before they happened.

Strategy 2: The Competitive Intelligence Mining

Your customers talk about competitors. AI listens.

Prompt to use: "In this feedback, identify any mentions of competitors or alternatives:

- Direct mentions: [competitor names]
- Indirect mentions: [switching, shopping around, comparing]
- Feature comparisons: [what they like elsewhere]

Extract:

1. Why customers consider alternatives
2. What specific features they want
3. Switching triggers to avoid
4. Competitive advantages we have but don't emphasize."

That prompt might reveal killer features customers loved but were never marketed. Making them front and center, the conversion rate could jump 23% or more.

Strategy 3: The Emotion-Outcome Correlation

Beyond what customers say, how they feel predicts what they'll do.

AI emotional analysis revealed:

- Frustrated customers who get a resolution become the biggest advocates
- Neutral satisfaction scores predict churn better than negative
- Excitement in feedback correlates with referrals
- Confusion predicts support costs

Restructure your support to create more "heroic recoveries." Watch your NPS (Net Promoter Score) go up significantly.

Transforming Insights into Stakeholder Gold

Having insights means nothing if nobody acts on them. Here's how to make stakeholders care:

The Executive Translation Engine

C-suite doesn't want data. They want decisions.

Try this stakeholder reporting prompt: "Transform this customer feedback analysis into executive insights:

Raw findings: [paste analysis] Business context: [current priorities] Financial implications: [relevant metrics]

Create:

1. One-page executive summary
2. Three key insights with business impact
3. Recommended actions with ROI estimates
4. Risk assessment of inaction
5. Quick wins vs. strategic initiatives

Write for someone with 5 minutes who controls the budget."

The Box AI Integration Success Story: Here's a masterclass in AI-driven business communication: Box's challenge: Multiple quarters of earnings calls where they needed to articulate their AI strategy effectively to investors. Clear communication about AI investments was crucial for market confidence.

Their AI approach:

- Integrated AI deeply into their core platform offerings
- Used AI partnerships with Anthropic, OpenAI, and Google to strengthen messaging
- Leveraged AI capabilities to demonstrate real business value
- Created new Enterprise Advanced tier specifically for AI use cases

Result: Strong investor confidence. Q1 2026 showed 4% revenue growth, 21% RPO growth, and 25.3% operating margins. Stock responded positively to clear AI strategy communication.

Your takeaway: AI doesn't just power products; when communicated effectively, it becomes a key driver of investor confidence and business growth. [3]

BUILDING YOUR INSIGHT-TO-ACTION PIPELINE

Week 1: Unify Your Feedback

Tools needed:

- **Zapier/Make**: Connect feedback sources
- **Airtable/Notion**: Central repository
- **ChatGPT/Claude**: Analysis engine

Action: Connect just TWO feedback sources first. Perfect the process, then expand.

Week 2: Generate First Insights

Daily practice:

- Feed batch of feedback to AI
- Ask for the top 3 insights
- Validate against your intuition
- Track predictions

Success metric: One "aha!" moment that changes a decision.

Week 3: Stakeholder Communication

Templates to create:

- Weekly insight email (3 bullets max)
- Monthly trend report (1 page)
- Quarterly strategic review (5 slides)
- Emergency issue alert (immediate action)

Test with one stakeholder first. Refine based on their feedback.

Week 4: Close the Loop

The critical step most miss:

- Track what changes get implemented
- Measure the impact of changes
- Feed results back to AI
- Show stakeholders the ROI

This creates a virtuous cycle of insight → action → results → more buy-in.

COMMON FEEDBACK ANALYSIS MISTAKES

Mistake 1: Surveying to Death

More surveys ≠ better insights.

Fix: Mine existing interactions before creating new touchpoints.

Mistake 2: Ignoring Silent Customers

Only hearing from extremes (lovers and haters).

Fix: AI behavioral analysis speaks for the silent majority.

Mistake 3: Analysis Paralysis

Perfect insights delivered too late.

Fix: 80% accurate insights weekly beat 100% accurate quarterly.

The Hidden Goldmine: Cross-Functional Intelligence

Here's one element that transformed our agency: connecting departmental feedback.

Sales knows why deals are lost. Support knows why customers struggle. Marketing knows what messages resonate.

But they rarely talk.

AI becomes your universal translator: "Analyze feedback from all departments:

- Sales: [lost deal reasons]
- Support: [common issues]
- Marketing: [campaign responses]

Find:

1. Disconnects between promise and delivery
2. Opportunities hiding between departments
3. Quick wins requiring cross-team coordination
4. Strategic advantages that we're not leveraging"

One client discovered that Sales was losing deals over a benefit that existed but marketing never mentioned. Fixed in one day. The closed rate improved by 18%.

Your Feedback Intelligence Checklist

Rate your current state:

Collection Excellence:

- [ ] Multiple feedback channels active
- [ ] Passive feedback captured
- [ ] Real-time collection systems
- [ ] Historical data preserved

Analysis Sophistication:

- [ ] Cross-channel pattern recognition
- [ ] Sentiment trajectory tracking
- [ ] Predictive modeling active
- [ ] Competitive intelligence extracted

Communication Effectiveness:

- [ ] Regular stakeholder updates
- [ ] Clear action recommendations
- [ ] ROI tracking on changes
- [ ] Feedback loop closed

Action Orientation:

- [ ] Insights drive decisions
- [ ] Changes implemented quickly
- [ ] Results measured consistently
- [ ] Success stories documented

Score below 12/16? You're sitting on untapped gold.

The One Feedback Question That Matters

"If we could only fix one thing based on customer feedback, what would create the most value?"

Not the loudest complaint. Not the easiest fix, but the highest impact change. AI helps you find it in the noise.

Your Intelligence Challenge

This week:

1. Pick your messiest feedback source
2. Feed it to AI with the master prompt
3. Find one insight you didn't know
4. Act on it immediately
5. Measure the impact

Start messy. Perfect later. Insights now.

Coming up: You've built incredible systems and gathered powerful insights. But what happens when key people leave? Chapter 12 reveals how AI transforms tribal knowledge into institutional intelligence.

CHAPTER 12
THE LEARNING LEGACY: CONVERTING CAMPAIGN EXPERIENCE INTO ORGANIZATIONAL INTELLIGENCE

"EVERYTHING SARAH KNEW JUST WALKED out the door." The startup founder's voice cracked. Sarah, their marketing director for three years, had just given notice. With her went:

- Which campaigns actually worked (and why)
- Relationships with key vendors
- The real story behind the numbers
- Countless lessons learned the hard way

Two months later, her replacement was making the same expensive mistakes Sarah had learned to avoid in year one.

Have you experienced this, too? Most businesses are one departure away from amnesia.

THE KNOWLEDGE CRISIS NOBODY DISCUSSES

Here's the uncomfortable truth: Your organization's most valuable asset walks out the door every night. Sometimes it doesn't come back.

At Smart Business Development, we lost our chief videographer/editor, who had been with us for two years. Their replacement took three months to reach 50% effectiveness. The knowledge gap cost us a major client.

That's when I realized we weren't running a business. We were renting expertise that could leave at any time.

THE THREE TYPES OF ORGANIZATIONAL KNOWLEDGE

Level 1: Documented Facts "We have SOPs!" (That nobody reads)

- Process documents
- Campaign reports
- Meeting notes
- Strategy decks

Level 2: Contextual Understanding "Veterans know the real story" (But never write it down)

- Why decisions were made
- What actually worked vs. looked good
- Relationships and politics
- Unwritten rules

Level 3: Evolutionary Intelligence "We learn and improve systematically" (The holy grail)

- Patterns across campaigns
- Predictive insights
- Institutional wisdom
- Self-improving systems

AI transforms Level 1 into Level 3 without depending on any individual.

Building Your Learning Intelligence System

Forget post-mortems that get filed and forgotten. Build systems that make every experience compound.

THE KNOWLEDGE CAPTURE FRAMEWORK

Traditional Approach: End-of-campaign report

- What: Dry recitation of facts
- When: Weeks after the campaign ends
- Who: Whoever has time
- Result: PDF nobody reads

AI-Enhanced Approach: Living intelligence system

- What: Real-time insight capture
- When: Continuously throughout the campaign
- Who: AI + human validation
- Result: Searchable, actionable intelligence

Here's how you build it:

Layer 1: Automatic Documentation

- All meetings recorded and transcribed
- Decisions tracked with context
- Results linked to actions
- Patterns identified across campaigns

Layer 2: Insight Extraction

- AI analyzes what worked/failed
- Identifies non-obvious connections
- Surfaces applicable lessons
- Predicts future application

Layer 3: Knowledge Activation

- Relevant insights surface automatically
- Past lessons inform current decisions
- Success patterns replicate
- Failure patterns avoided

The Post-Mortem Revolution

Traditional post-mortems are where insights go to die. AI brings them to life.

The Brutal Truth About Traditional Post-Mortems

I've sat through plenty. They usually go:

- Blame disguised as "lessons learned"
- Surface-level observations
- Political tap-dancing
- Filed and forgotten

Why? Because humans protecting relationships avoid hard truths.

The AI Post-Mortem Advantage

AI doesn't care about office politics. It finds truth in data.

Try this post-mortem prompt: "Analyze this campaign data objectively:

- Goals vs. results: [data]
- Timeline and milestones: [data]
- Resource allocation: [data]
- Team communications: [data]
- Customer feedback: [data]

Identify:

1. Root causes of success/failure (not symptoms)
2. Decisions that had an outsized impact
3. Patterns matching previous campaigns

4. Predictive indicators we missed
5. Specific improvements for next time

Focus on systems and processes, not individuals."

Mintel's Knowledge Transformation

Mintel's sales teams had a problem: With over 6,000 global clients, data patterns in calls weren't easy to spot. Great reps excelled. New reps struggled. Knowledge stayed siloed across regions.

Their AI solution:

- Gong recorded and transcribed every sales call
- AI analyzed successful vs. unsuccessful conversations
- Identified winning talk tracks and client engagement patterns
- Created a searchable knowledge base of best practices
- Enabled peer-to-peer learning from top performers

Results:

- Win rates: Up 34% since implementation
- Coaching culture: Established across all teams
- Knowledge transfer: Accelerated for new initiatives
- Remote coaching: Made more effective globally
- Self-coaching: Enabled through data-driven insights

The key? They didn't just capture what happened. They used AI to identify why certain approaches worked and scaled those insights across their entire global sales organization. [1]

ADVANCED LEARNING STRATEGIES

Strategy 1: The Pattern Library Build

Don't just record campaigns. Map patterns.

This was built for an e-commerce client:

- Every campaign tagged with 50+ attributes
- AI identifies correlation patterns
- Success formulas emerge
- Failure patterns become warnings

Discovery: Campaigns launched on Tuesdays with video content and urgency messaging had a 73% higher ROI. Nobody knew why, but the pattern was undeniable.

Strategy 2: The Failure Forensics Deep Dive

Winners teach confidence. Failures teach competence.

Try this failure analysis prompt: "This campaign failed to meet goals. Analyze:

- Original hypothesis and assumptions
- Early warning signals we missed
- Decision points where we could have pivoted
- External vs. internal factors
- How to spot this pattern earlier next time

Be brutally honest. Assume good intentions but flawed execution."

Turned our biggest flop into a checklist that prevented five similar failures.

Strategy 3: The Knowledge Democracy

Best insights often come from unexpected sources.

AI-powered insight democracy:

- Anyone can submit observations
- AI validates against data
- Patterns across submissions identified
- Best insights bubble up regardless of the source

When I was designing, I noticed that our highest-converting ads featured models who were looking at the offer or product. Seemed random until eye tracking confirmed: people looked at eyes of models to see what they were looking at. Turns out that humans naturally follow another person's line of sight. This produced a 23% higher CTR across 200 campaigns.

INDUSTRY LEADERS IN KNOWLEDGE PRESERVATION

ilert: Automated post-mortem platform that eliminates human bias. Their AI analyzes incident data objectively, creating consistent reports that actually get used.

Zenduty: 50% reduction in resolution time by turning every incident into a learning opportunity. AI identifies root causes and prevents repeat issues.

Atlassian + AI: Their Confluence platform now uses AI to make documentation searchable and relevant. Static wikis become dynamic knowledge.

Stack Overflow for Teams: AI-powered deduplication and recommendation. Stops the same questions from being asked 100 times.

Pattern: Leaders treat knowledge as a living asset, not static documentation.

BUILDING YOUR LEARNING ORGANIZATION

Phase 1: Capture Everything (Month 1)

Tools needed:

- **Otter.ai/Grain**: Meeting transcription
- **Loom**: Process documentation
- **Notion/Confluence**: Central repository

Start simple:

- Record important meetings
- Document decisions with context

- Save campaign assets systematically
- Tag everything religiously

Phase 2: Extract Intelligence (Month 2)

Weekly practice:

- Feed week's documentation to AI
- Extract key decisions and outcomes
- Identify patterns and connections
- Update team on insights

Success metric: One "I didn't know that" moment weekly.

Phase 3: Activate Knowledge (Month 3)

Build the bridges:

- Create "Before you start" checklists
- Surface relevant past campaigns
- Automate lesson reminders
- Track implementation of insights

The test: Can a new hire find everything they need without asking?

Phase 4: Compound Learning (Ongoing)

The flywheel effect:

- Every campaign adds to intelligence
- Patterns become more predictive
- Decisions get more informed
- Results improve systematically

This is how organizations become truly intelligent.

COMMON KNOWLEDGE MANAGEMENT MISTAKES

Mistake 1: Documentation Theater

Creating documents that nobody uses.

Fix: Focus on searchability and relevance over completeness.

Mistake 2: Information Hoarding

Knowledge as power leads to silos.

Fix: Reward knowledge sharing and make hoarding impossible.

Mistake 3: One-Time Captures

Post-mortems at campaign end only.

Fix: Continuous capture throughout your campaign lifecycle.

The Psychology of Organizational Learning

Here's what 20 years taught me: Organizations don't learn; people do. But people leave.

AI can help you create institutional memory that:

- Survives personnel changes
- Improves with every iteration
- Surfaces at the right moment
- Evolves beyond any individual

When Sarah left that startup, version 2.0 would have:

- Every campaign she ran is analyzed
- Every decision is documented with context
- Every relationship is mapped and maintained
- Every lesson is preserved and accessible

Her replacement would start at 80% effectiveness, not 0%.

Your Knowledge Preservation Audit

Score your current state:

Capture Completeness:

- [ ] Key meetings recorded
- [ ] Decisions documented with context
- [ ] Campaign assets organized
- [ ] Results linked to actions

Intelligence Extraction:

- [ ] Regular pattern analysis
- [ ] Cross-campaign insights
- [ ] Predictive indicators tracked
- [ ] Failure forensics conducted

Knowledge Activation:

- [ ] Searchable repository
- [ ] Onboarding uses past insights
- [ ] Decisions reference history
- [ ] Lessons actually implemented

Continuous Improvement:

- [ ] Every campaign adds to knowledge
- [ ] Patterns increasingly predictive
- [ ] Team actively contributes
- [ ] System evolves automatically

Score below 12/16? Your organization has amnesia.

THE KNOWLEDGE TRANSFORMATION ROADMAP

Week 1: Stop the Bleeding

- Pick one critical process
- Document it completely
- Include context and decisions
- Make it searchable

Week 2: Mine the Past

- Gather the last 6 months of campaigns
- Feed to AI for pattern analysis
- Document surprising insights
- Share with team

Week 3: Build the System

- Choose knowledge platform
- Create capture templates
- Set up AI analysis
- Train your team on the process

Week 4: Activate Intelligence

- Surface insights in planning
- Reference past lessons
- Track implementation
- Measure impact

The One Knowledge Question That Matters

"If our best performer left tomorrow, what would we lose forever?"

Now, systematically capture that knowledge before they leave.

Your Learning Challenge

This week:

1. Record one important meeting
2. Feed transcript to AI
3. Extract three insights
4. Document with context
5. Share with your team

Start building institutional memory today.

The Ultimate Marketing Transformation

Congratulations. You've journeyed through the complete AI marketing transformation:

- From guessing to knowing (Research)
- From generic to memorable (Positioning)
- From funnel to journey (Architecture)
- From content scarcity to abundance (Creation)
- From spray to precision (Channels)
- From leads to relationships (Generation)
- From chaos to coordination (Launches)
- From metrics to insights (Analytics)
- From growth to scale (Expansion)
- From churn to champions (Retention)
- From data to decisions (Intelligence)
- From knowledge to wisdom (Learning)

But this isn't the end. It's your beginning.

Coming up: How do you implement all of this without losing your soul? Chapter 13 reveals the ethical framework for AI marketing that builds trust while driving results.

CHAPTER 13
ETHICAL CONSIDERATIONS AND DATA PRIVACY: USING AI RESPONSIBLY

"WE NEED to talk about the campaign." The legal counsel's tone makes your stomach drop. Your client's AI-powered personalization campaign achieved incredible results, with a 47% increase in conversions and customers raving about the relevant content. But now legal has concerns.

"Some customers are asking how we knew they were interested in that specific product. They feel like we're reading their minds. Or worse, spying on them."

That conversation will quickly change how you think about AI in marketing. Power without responsibility isn't just unethical; it's bad business.

THE TRUST EQUATION THAT CHANGES EVERYTHING

Here's what takes too many marketers too long to learn: In the age of AI, trust is your only sustainable competitive advantage.

Technology? Competitors will copy it. Tactics? They'll spread industry-wide. Trust? Once broken, it is nearly impossible to rebuild.

THE THREE PILLARS OF ETHICAL AI MARKETING

- **Pillar 1: Transparency -** People have a right to know
- **Pillar 2: Value Exchange -** Both parties should benefit
- **Pillar 3: Human Control -** AI assists while humans decide

If you miss any pillar, then you're building on sand.

Pillar 1: Radical Transparency in the Age of AI

Transparency isn't about legal compliance. It's about human respect.

The Transparency Framework

Level 1: Minimum Legal "We use AI" (buried on page 47 of Terms)

Level 2: Checkbox Compliance "This content was AI-generated" (tiny footer text)

Level 3: Authentic Transparency "Here's exactly how we use AI to help you, and here's how to control it."

Guess which level builds lasting relationships?

Practical Transparency Implementation

Here's your new transparency checklist:

Data Collection:

- Explain what you collect in plain English
- Show why each data point helps the customer
- Provide easy opt-out without penalty
- Regular reminders about data use

AI Use Disclosure:

- Clear indicators when AI is involved
- Explanation of AI's role vs. human role
- Options to request human-only interaction
- Transparency report published quarterly

Real Case Study: Spotify's "Why This Song?" Feature

Implementation: Spotify added transparent "Why This Song?" labels to their Discover Weekly and Daily Mix playlists with hover explanations: "This recommendation is based on your listening history and similar user preferences. Click to adjust your music taste profile."

Result? User trust in AI recommendations increased 85%. Playlist engagement improved with the trust-satisfaction model, showing 5% better performance when transparency features were included. [1]

The LEGO Standard

Want to see transparency done right? Look at LEGO's approach to children's data:

- Plain language that kids can understand
- Parents control everything
- Data deleted automatically
- Regular communication about changes

They exceed legal requirements. Result? Parents trust them completely. That trust drives billions in sales.

Pillar 2: The Value Exchange Economy

Every piece of data has a price. Are you paying it?

The Data-Value Balance Sheet

Old Model: Take data and deliver ads.

New Model: Exchange data for genuine value

Example from our research:

Fitness App Company:

- Asks for: Daily activity data
- Delivers: Personalized workout plans that actually work
- Result: 89% user retention

Travel Site Company:

- Asks for: Past trip preferences
- Delivers: Curated destinations they'd never find alone
- Result: 5x repeat booking rate

The pattern? When the value exceeds intrusion, customers gladly participate.

Algorithmic Bias: The Hidden Ethics Killer

Here's an uncomfortable truth: AI amplifies existing biases unless actively prevented.

Real scenario: Financial services client's AI consistently offered lower credit limits to women. Not programmed bias, learned from historical data where humans had been biased.

Try This Bias Prevention Protocol:

1. **Diverse Training Data**: Actively balance datasets
2. **Regular Audits**: Test outputs across demographics
3. **Human Review**: Flag anomalies for investigation
4. **Transparent Appeals**: Clear process for customers

Try this prompt for bias checking: "Analyze these AI outputs for potential bias: [Sample outputs across demographics]

Check for:

1. Systematic differences in recommendations
2. Language tone variations
3. Offer quality disparities
4. Access to features/benefits

Flag any patterns that could indicate unfair treatment."

Pillar 3: Maintaining Human Control

AI should amplify human judgment, not replace it.

The Decision Hierarchy

AI Handles:

- Data processing
- Pattern recognition
- Initial recommendations
- Routine responses

Humans Handle:

- Ethical judgments
- Exception cases
- Relationship building
- Final decisions

Together They:

- Create better outcomes
- Maintain accountability
- Build trust
- Scale responsibly

Real-World Application

Customer Service Example:

- AI suggests a response based on the type of issue
- Human reviews for appropriateness
- AI personalizes language
- Human adds empathy and judgment
- AI ensures follow-up
- Human maintains relationship

Result: 70% faster resolution, 94% satisfaction rate.

INDUSTRY-SPECIFIC ETHICAL CONSIDERATIONS

Voice Technology: The Uncanny Valley

AI voice technology has become so lifelike it's scary. Literally.

Ethical Requirements:

- Always disclose AI voice use
- Never clone without explicit permission
- Clear AI indicators in conversation
- Easy transfer to human option

If you intend to use AI to automate outbound calling, I urge you to check your Federal and State laws that restrict AI use. Fines are extremely high.

A lead gen company I worked for used AI for outbound cold calling in a different way. They hired offshore cold callers to make live calls but then used AI to make them sound American. If you use AI voice technology in your customer support to handle inbound calls, then try starting every call with "Hi, I'm Alex, an AI assistant. I can help with basic questions or connect you with a human anytime."

Transparency can reduce hang-ups by 67% or more.

Generative Content: The Authenticity Challenge

When AI creates content indistinguishable from human-made content, authenticity questions arise.

Our Content Ethics Framework:

- AI assists, humans create
- Always maintain brand voice
- Fact-check everything
- Add human experiences
- Disclose when appropriate

Example: This book was written with AI assistance. But every personal story, every insight, every decision comes from my human experience. AI helped me research case studies and write faster, not think differently. I used Grammarly to help me edit this book, but I chose every comma, period, and semicolon.

Predictive Analytics: The Minority Report Problem

Predicting behavior can feel creepy. Or helpful. The difference? Implementation.

Creepy: "We know you're about to cancel, so here's a discount."

Helpful: "Based on your goals, you might enjoy this new feature."

Same prediction. Different application. Vastly different customer response.

BUILDING YOUR ETHICAL AI FRAMEWORK

Step 1: Define Your Principles

Start with questions:

- What would we want as customers?
- What would we tell our kids?
- What builds long-term trust?
- What feels right, not just legal?

Document answers as your ethical foundation.

Step 2: Implement Practical Safeguards

Technical Safeguards:

- Data minimization (collect only what you need)
- Encryption everywhere
- Regular deletion schedules
- Access controls and audit logs

Process Safeguards:

- Human review requirements
- Bias testing protocols
- Customer control panels
- Regular ethical audits

Cultural Safeguards:

- Ethics training for all team members
- Reward ethical decisions
- Safe reporting channels
- Learn from mistakes openly

Step 3: Measure What Matters

Track trust metrics:

- Consent rates (real choice, not forced)
- Opt-out rates (are people comfortable?)
- Trust survey scores
- Ethics-related support tickets
- Long-term customer value

High trust = high LTV. Every time.

COMMON ETHICAL PITFALLS

Pitfall 1: The Boiling Frog

Starting ethically, then slowly pushing boundaries.

Prevention: Regular ethical audits. Ask, "Would we do this on day one?"

Pitfall 2: The Echo Chamber

Only considering your perspective.

Prevention: Diverse team input. Customer advisory boards. External ethics review.

Pitfall 3: The Competition Excuse

"Everyone else is doing it."

Prevention: Define your standards. Compete on trust, not tricks.

The Business Case for Ethics

Let's talk ROI because ethics isn't just right; it's profitable:

Trust Premium: Customers pay 17% more to companies they trust (PwC study)

Retention Boost: Transparent companies see 23% higher retention.

Referral Power: Trusted brands get 3x more word-of-mouth.

Risk Reduction: Avoid fines, lawsuits, and PR disasters.

Talent Magnet: 86% of employees prefer ethical employers.

Ethics isn't a cost center. It's a profit driver.

Your Ethical AI Checklist

Before launching any AI marketing:

Transparency:

- [ ] Clear disclosure of AI use
- [ ] Plain English privacy policy
- [ ] Visible opt-out options
- [ ] Regular communication

Value Exchange:

- [ ] Clear benefit to customer
- [ ] Fair data-for-value trade
- [ ] Respect for preferences
- [ ] Genuine utility provided

Bias Prevention:

- [ ] Diverse training data
- [ ] Regular output audits
- [ ] Appeal processes
- [ ] Human oversight

Control:

- [ ] Customer data access
- [ ] Modification options
- [ ] Deletion rights
- [ ] Human alternatives

Score 16/16 or fix what's missing.

The Future of Ethical AI Marketing

The companies winning tomorrow are building ethical foundations today:

- Apple: Privacy as a product feature
- Patagonia: Transparency as brand value
- LEGO: Protection as a promise

They prove ethics and success aren't opposites; they're partners.

Your Ethical Challenge

This week:

1. Audit one AI marketing system for ethics
2. Find one place you're prioritizing efficiency over transparency
3. Fix it
4. Measure customer response
5. Share results with your team

Start small. Build habits. Create culture.

The One Ethics Question That Matters

"Would I want my family to be marketed to this way?"

If the answer is no, you know what to do.

Final Thoughts: Your AI Marketing Journey

We've covered a lot of ground together:

- From manual research to AI insights
- From generic messaging to memorable positioning
- From broken funnels to intelligent journeys
- From content scarcity to strategic abundance
- From channel chaos to focused dominance
- From lead generation to relationship building
- From launch panic to coordinated execution
- From data overload to actionable intelligence
- From linear growth to exponential scaling
- From customer churn to lifetime advocates
- From feedback noise to strategic insights
- From tribal knowledge to institutional intelligence
- From AI wild west to ethical leadership

But knowledge without action is just entertainment.

YOUR NEXT STEP

Pick one chapter. One challenge you're facing right now. Implement one AI solution this week.

Start small. Build momentum. Transform your marketing.

The robots aren't coming for your job. They're here to help you do it better than you ever imagined possible.

Welcome to the future of marketing. It's time to build something amazing.

Remember: AI is just a tool. You're the strategist. Together, you're unstoppable.

Now, go forth and revolutionize your marketing. I'll be cheering you on,

Brian

P.S. When you achieve that first AI-powered win, I'd love to hear about it. Please, email me at Brian@DuvallConsulting.com. Your success stories will inspire others.

Pass the Torch Forward

Now that you've discovered how to streamline your marketing with AI, escape the content creation hamster wheel, and actually see results from your campaigns, you hold something powerful: knowledge that could transform another marketer's life.

Remember that overwhelming feeling from Chapter 1? The late nights staring at blank screens? The panic of impossible deadlines? Someone else is living that nightmare right now. But you can throw them a lifeline.

Your honest review on Amazon becomes a beacon for marketers who are:

- Googling "marketing automation" at 2 AM
- Wondering if AI is just hype or actual help
- Desperate for a way to do more without burning out
- Ready to grow but stuck in manual processes

Think back to where you were before reading this book. What would you have wanted someone to tell you? That's exactly what your review can do for the next reader.

Here's the thing about our marketing community: We succeed when we share what works. Every time you've learned a killer strategy, discovered a game-changing tool or found a shortcut that saved your sanity, it probably came from another marketer paying it forward.

Now it's your turn to keep that chain going.

Your review doesn't need to be fancy. Just share:

- What problem this book solved for you
- One "aha!" moment that changed your approach
- Whether you'd recommend it (and to whom)
- How it impacted your daily work

Marketing careers thrive when we lift each other up. By sharing your experience, you're not just leaving a review; you're potentially saving someone from giving up on their dreams.

Thank you for keeping our community strong. Every career you help transform makes our entire industry better.

To your success (and theirs),

Brian Duvall

P.S. If even one chapter in this book made your work life easier, imagine what your review could do for someone who's about to throw in the towel. Sometimes, the right book at the right time can change everything. Help someone find theirs.

BONUS 1:

I have put all the prompts in this book online for you at https://brianduvall.com/ai-marketing-prompts-reference-guide

Simply copy and paste the prompts into your favorite AI platform, add in your specific data and details, then let AI do its thing.

BONUS 2:

I have also put all the AI tools and platforms mentioned in this book online for you at https://brianduvall.com/ai-marketing-tools-reference-guide

Each tool is categorized by use type for quick and easy reference.

Ready to help a fellow marketer find their breakthrough?
Scan this QR Code to leave your review on Amazon

NOTES

AI MARKETING MATURITY MODEL

1. SuperAGI, "How AI-driven sales automation increased conversion rates by 20%," 2025.
2. Chiancone, C., "Case study successes: How top law firms are implementing AI." 2023.

1. STREAMLINING MARKET RESEARCH WITH AI TOOLS

1. Zonka Feedback, "AI customer feedback analysis: The key to unlock customer intelligence," May 23, 2025.
2. Qatalog, "How AI is transforming consumer insights for a global electronics brand," January 10, 2024.

2. MASTERING BRAND POSITIONING WITH AI TOOLS

1. Brand.ai, "Brand.ai uses AI to make brands more human with Claude," December 18, 2024.
2. Cut the SaaS, "Beauty and the bot: How Sephora reimagined customer experience with AI," 2024.

3. OPTIMIZING SALES FUNNELS WITH AI TECHNOLOGY

1. Pylon, "How AI-powered customer support reduces response times by 97% and achieves 50% automated resolution rates with real case studies," June 12, 2025.
2. Growth Hackers, "Marketing automation case study: How we leveraged the power of AI and automation to build an automated sales funnel," March 2, 2025.
3. Demand Gen Report, "AI's role in optimizing the marketing funnel," April 16, 2024.
4. Aptivio, "Capgemini case study - AI powered revenue growth," n.d.
5. VKTR, "5 AI case studies in sales: ACI Corporation and Salesken," March 26, 2024.
6. Adstra, "The sales funnel is dead. The AI sales funnel is here," March 3, 2025.
7. Trustmary, "Case Studies," 2022.
8. SmartAsset, "Tax Savings Calculator," 2025.
9. Cog Dental, "Dental marketing case study: Crafting a full-funnel strategy from awareness to booking," n.d.

4. TRANSFORMING CONTENT CREATION WITH AI TOOLS

1. LinkedIn Business Solutions, "AI in B2B: Going beyond the hype," n.d.
2. TheB2Bmarketer, "AI-powered personalisation transforms lead nurturing at Ingersoll," May 6, 2025.

3. Matrix Marketing Group, "AI content planning for manufacturing companies: Steel-Sync Solutions boosts engagement with personalization," September 9, 2024.
4. SuperAGI, "Optimizing your sales funnel with AI: A case study on how AI native companies outperform their peers," June 28, 2025.
5. Geeks For Growth, "The dental practice makeover guide – Transform your patient experience, brand, website & local SEO for real growth," June 11, 2025.

5. WINNING THE CHANNEL GAME WITH AI STRATEGY

1. SparkOptimus, "Building and operating a new digital-first venture: Heineken's Beerwulf," n.d.
2. Olo, "Slim Chickens | Olo case study," 2024.
3. The Weather Company, "Weather targeting: AI-driven, hyperlocal weather-based advertising," 2025.
4. Menuboard Manager, "AI-Powered Menu Boards adapt to customer behavior, personalize picks, adjust based on time and weather," June 21, 2024.
5. Dillon, S., "Not just for teens - TikTok means business for Kenney Property Services," August 21, 2020.
6. Mighty Moxie Marketing, Why law firms need to use social media," December 1, 2024.

6. AUTOMATING SUCCESS: THE AI LEAD GENERATION REVOLUTION

1. Unbounce, "How hyper-targeted marketing helped Zola change the wedding industry with over 300 landing pages," June 7, 2024.
2. Bibit.ai, "AI-Powered Lead Nurturing: 7 Automated Email Sequences That Convert Cold Prospects into Hot Buyers in 2025," July 26, 2025.
3. Leadzen.ai. "AISDR | AI-powered sales development representative," 2025.

7. THE COUNTDOWN BEGINS: LAUNCHING WITH AI PRECISION

1. Mars Wrigley, "Mars Wrigley cites 67% sales lift from Amazon Australia personalisation campaign," May 21, 2025.
2. Young Urban Project, "6 best AI marketing case studies," 2025.
3. Inc., B. M., "Nutella 'hired' an algorithm to design new jars. And it was a sell out." June 5, 2017.
4. Rethink Canada, "Heinz: A.I. Ketchup campaign," 2023.
5. The Coca-Cola Company, "Groundbreaking digital experience and films fuse holiday heritage with cutting-edge tech," October 12, 2024.

8. THE OPTIMIZATION SYMPHONY: ORCHESTRATING SUCCESS WITH AI ANALYTICS

1. Agile Growth Labs, "How brands like Unilever and Delta are using AI to go viral," July 17, 2025.
2. eWeek, "BMW and IBM collaborate to develop AI-driven personalized vehicle experience," December 15, 2016.

3. DigitalDefynd, "10 ways Coca-Cola is using AI - Case study," April 4, 2025.

9. THE SCALING STRATOSPHERE: ACCELERATING GROWTH WITH AI INTELLIGENCE

1. Ferguson, M., "StackBlitz rises: From near failure to AI-powered success with Bolt.new," May 18, 2025.
2. Ferguson, M., "Anysphere's AI-code editor Cursor fastest to reach $100M ARR in 12 months." March 13, 2025.
3. Tian, J., "Midjourney ARR at $500M with 40 people?" February 21, 2025.
4. Sacra, "ElevenLabs revenue, valuation & growth rate," May 31, 2025.
5. Maisuria, C., "Notion's product-led growth (PLG) growth strategy: From 0 to $10 billion," June 15, 2021.
6. HireVue, "AI in recruiting: Ethical & effective AI hiring," n.d.

10. THE LOYALTY LABORATORY: ENGINEERING RETENTION WITH AI INTELLIGENCE

1. Pecan AI., "We used AI to predict customer churn - now what? Churn reduction initiatives," June 18, 2024.
2. Anthropic, "How Intercom achieves 86% resolution rates with Claude AI: A customer service revolution," n.d.
3. Netflix Technology Blog, "Netflix recommender system - A big data case study," 2021.

11. THE INSIGHT SYMPHONY: ORCHESTRATING FEEDBACK AND COMMUNICATION WITH AI ANALYTICS

1. SentiSum, "How Scandinavian Biolabs use SentiSum to reprioritise product roadmaps and identify churn drivers," n.d.
2. Nort Labs, "Costa Coffee automation case study," July 13, 2024.
3. Insider Monkey, "Box, Inc. (NYSE:BOX) Q1 2026 earnings call transcript," May 28, 2025.

12. THE LEARNING LEGACY: CONVERTING CAMPAIGN EXPERIENCE INTO ORGANIZATIONAL INTELLIGENCE

1. Gong, "Mintel's achieve 34% win rate increase | Gong case study," February 5, 2025.

13. ETHICAL CONSIDERATIONS AND DATA PRIVACY: USING AI RESPONSIBLY

1. El-Adaileh, N. A., & Foster, S., "The moderating role of personalized recommendations in the trust–satisfaction–loyalty relationship: An empirical study of AI-driven e-commerce," 2025

Made in United States
Troutdale, OR
11/03/2026

56852696R00114